A

Trails Guide
Colorado
Central Mountains

By CHARLES A. WELLS

Author at Webster Pass on Trail #20. Radical Hill, Trail #19, in background.

Easy • Moderate • Difficult
ATV Riding Adventures

FunTreks, Inc.

Published by FunTreks, Inc.
P. O. Box 3127, Monument, CO 80132-3127
Phone: Toll Free 877-222-7623, Fax: 719-277-7411
E-mail: books@funtreks.com
Web site: www.funtreks.com

Edited by Shelley Mayer
Cover design, photography, maps, and production by Charles A. Wells

First Edition, Third Printing

Library of Congress Control Number 2007921536
ISBN 978-0-9664976-9-4

Printed in China.

To order additional books, call toll-free 1-877-222-7623 or use order form in back of this
book. You may also order online at www.funtreks.com.

TRAIL UPDATES:
For latest trail updates and changes, check the *Trails Updates* page on our Web site at
www.funtreks.com.

GUARANTEE OF SATISFACTION:
If you are dissatisfied with this book in any way, please call our toll-free number during
business hours at 1-877-222-7623. We promise to do whatever it takes to make you
happy.

DISCLAIMER

Travel in Colorado's backcountry is, by its very nature, potentially dangerous and could result in property damage, injury, or even death. The scope
of this book cannot predict every possible hazard you may encounter. If you
ride any of the trails in this book, you acknowledge these risks and assume
full responsibility. You are the final judge as to whether a trail is safe to ride
on any given day, whether your vehicle is capable of the journey and what
supplies you should carry. The information contained herein cannot replace
good judgment and proper preparation on your part. The publisher and
author of this book disclaim any and all liability for bodily injury, death, or
property damage that could occur to you or any fellow travelers.

At the time this book was written, all routes were legal for OHV use.
However, new forest plans could change route designation in the future. It
is your responsibility to be aware of these changes when or if they occur.
(See page 16 for more details.)

ACKNOWLEDGMENTS

My sincere thanks to the following individuals and organizations who helped with this book:

The U.S. Forest Service, Bureau of Land Management and Colorado State Parks. I worked with many hard-working staffers who provided courteous and professional advice.

Dudley Fecht, long-time resident of Buena Vista and avid rider of dirt bikes and ATVs. Dudley guided me on trails around Buena Vista and introduced me to several routes I'd never ridden, including the Otto Mears Toll Road, Fourmile South Area, Taylor Park and Texas Creek OHV Area.

David Wortman, instructor for the ATV Safety Institute in Aurora, CO. David was my safety class instructor and also guided me on trails in the Rainbow Falls OHV Area.

Dan Delasantos, active OHV enthusiast and long-time promoter of the sport. Dan is on the board of directors for COHVCO and the steering committee for the *Stay the Trail* campaign. Some may recognize his name as a journalist for *Sand Sport Magazine*. Dan shared his broad knowledge of statewide ATV activities and helped with trail selection.

Duke Sumonia, aviation archeologist, provided extensive information on the T-33 plane crash (Trail #9), including newspaper clippings and the chilling 40-year-old military accident report.

Chris Tori, serious ATV rider and sales representative for Xtreme Performance in Castle Rock, CO. Chris sold me two ATVs and shared many tips that helped on the trail.

Jason Schmidt and Ethan Remington of the Washington Adventure Quads, who showed me what extreme ATV riding is all about.

Ron Gardner, Dan Schaeffer, Joe Chacon, Brian Burbank, Kyle Carlisle, Mark Holley, Jim Haselden and John Kreikemeier, whose paths I crossed while out on the trails. They took time to share advice or ride with me so I could shoot their pictures.

Shelley Mayer, for her thorough editing of this book, Joan Aaland, who keeps our office running smoothly, my daughter, Marcia LeVault, for her marketing and administration support, and my wife, Beverly, without whom FunTreks would not be in business.

First Twin Trestle on Rollins Pass West, Trail #11. (Hiking only, closed to traffic.)

CONTENTS

Trail List

*Author's Favorites

Trail Locator Map

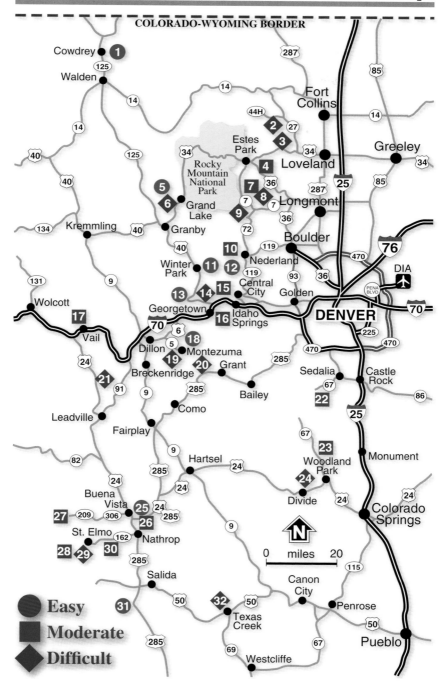

Trails Listed by Difficulty

Although trails are grouped into three major categories, there are still differences in difficulty within each group. For example, Red & White Mountain is easier than Mt. Antero even though both are rated moderate. Trails are progressively more difficult as you pan down the list, although you may have to skip several trails to see any significant difference.

No.	Trail	Page	Rating	Highest Pt.
5.	Stillwater Pass Road	46	Easy	10,500 ft.
12.	Rollins Pass East	74	Easy	11,800 ft.
13.	Jones Pass	78	Easy	12,500 ft.
11.	Rollins Pass West	70	Easy	11,700 ft.
25.	Fourmile North	126	Easy	9,200 ft.
18.	Peru Creek	98	Easy	11,900 ft.
31.	Otto Mears Toll Road	150	Easy	11,300 ft.
1.	North Sand Hills	30	Easy	8,500 ft.
17.	Red & White Mountain	94	Mod.	10,900 ft.
4.	Pole Hill	42	Mod.	8,900 ft.
26.	Fourmile South	130	Mod.	9,600 ft.
10.	Caribou, Eldorado Mountain	66	Mod.	10,200 ft.
23.	Rainbow Falls OHV Area	118	Mod.	8,800 ft.
28.	Tincup/Hancock Loop	138	Mod.	12,300 ft.
22.	Rampart Range OHV Area	114	Mod.	8,600 ft.
7.	Pierson Park Road	54	Mod.	9,400 ft.
16.	Saxon Mountain, Lamartine	90	Mod.	11,200 ft.
15.	Yankee Hill, Kingston Peak	86	Mod.	12,100 ft.
27.	Taylor Park	134	Mod.	10,300 ft.
30.	Mt. Antero, Baldwin Lakes	146	Mod.	13,800 ft.
21.	Camp Hale Area	110	Diff.	11,900 ft.
8.	Johnny Park Road	58	Diff.	8,500 ft.
14.	Bill Moore Lake, Empire Loop	82	Diff.	11,500 ft.
9.	Plane Crash, Ironclads	62	Diff.	8,900 ft.
2.	Moody Hill	34	Diff.	9,700 ft.
3.	Storm Mountain	38	Diff.	9,800 ft.
19.	Wise Mountain, Radical Hill	102	Diff.	12,600 ft.
29.	Pomeroy Lakes	142	Diff.	12,100 ft.
24.	North Divide 717 OHV Area	122	Diff.	9,200 ft.
6.	Idleglen OHV Area	50	Diff.	10,500 ft.
20.	Red Cone, Handcart Gulch	106	Diff.	12,800 ft.
32.	Texas Creek	154	Diff.	8,700 ft.

Trail Ratings Defined

Trail ratings are very subjective. Conditions change for many reasons, including weather and time of year. An easy trail can quickly become difficult when washed out by a rainstorm or blocked by a fallen rock. You must be the final judge of a trail's condition on the day you ride it. If any part of a trail is difficult, the entire trail is rated difficult. You may be able to ride a significant portion of a trail before reaching the difficult spot. Read each trail description carefully for specific information. Turn around when in doubt. Always wear a helmet.

● Easy Trails

Gravel, dirt, clay, sand, or mildly rocky trail or road. Gentle grades. Water levels low except during periods of heavy runoff. Adequate room to pass. Where shelf conditions exist, trail is wide and well maintained with minor sideways tilt. Most trails are passable when wet; however, certain types of clay can become impassable under wet conditions. Smaller, two-wheel-drive ATVs are usually adequate in good weather. Easy trails are best suited for novice riders.

■ Moderate Trails

Rougher and rockier surfaces require slower running speeds. Some riding experience is needed for steeper climbs and descents. Rock-stacking may be necessary to get over the worst spots. Considerable weight shifting may be necessary to offset sideways tilt. Mud can be deep and you may get stuck. Certain types of clay can become impassable when wet. Sand can be soft and steep. Water may be too deep for smaller ATVs. Larger ATVs can usually get through except during periods of heavy runoff. Aggressive tires needed for two-wheel-drive machines. Four-wheel-drive is usually best.

◆ Difficult Trails

Very rough and rocky surfaces require careful tire placement. Slopes may be extremely steep with scary sideways tilt. Skillful riding is necessary to avoid tipping or flipping over. Rock-stacking may be necessary in places, and the worst spots could require assistance from other people. Sand can be very soft and steep. Shelf roads can be very narrow with daunting cliffs. Water and mud can be very deep. Wet clay surfaces can be impassable. Some powerful two-wheel-drive ATVs may get through under good weather conditions, but four-wheel-drive with low-range gearing is highly recommended.

Rider nears top of Mt. Antero, Trail #30. (Elevation above 13,000 ft.)

INTRODUCTION

With so many people riding ATVs these days, you would think it would be easy to find great places to ride, especially here in Colorado. If you have just bought an ATV or have been riding a while, you have probably discovered the process is not so easy. There's a lot of information available, but it takes a while to sift through it all. The first time you go out, you might get lucky and have a great time, or you might come home disappointed.

I chuckle when I hear people say everything you need is on the Web. I've spent many hours online investigating trails and find most of the information very sketchy or, in many cases, just plain wrong, especially when it comes to directions. I'm in a better position than most people to evaluate because I've been to most of the places. Having written 10 books on back country trails in the last 12 years, I have a pretty good handle on what's out there.

Maps, of course, are most people's primary source of information. You really can't get along without them even with a good book like this. Maps show you the big picture, topographic details and how all the trails are tied together. But maps don't show you what's on the ground, what's around the next corner. More often than not, when you get there, you find the trails are not what you expected. Maps are notoriously inaccurate and out of date. Some forest maps haven't been updated in decades. The best maps, like *National Geographic* and *Latitude 40°,* are updated often. If you can find one of these maps for the area you're visiting, buy it. I have a closet full.

A few guidebooks for ATVs are already on the market, but most are just a collection of maps with basic directions to general areas. Once on the trail, you're on your own. Still, if the author has ridden the trails himself, the books can be helpful. The worst guidebooks are written by someone who has never been to the location described. He sits at a desk looking at a map, guessing at what's out there. If you've ever used a book like that, it doesn't take long to realize you've been hoodwinked. Of course, the cost to produce a book like that is much less than what I have to spend to ride all the trails.

I didn't start out riding ATVs; that has only happened the last three years. I started with four-wheel-drive SUVs, then got into Jeeping. I couldn't find any good guide books, so I decided to write one myself. Using the same methodology of driving all the routes myself, my first book, *Guide to Colorado Backroads & 4-Wheel Drive Trails,* sold very well. I think everyone else was looking for the same thing I was.

Right from the beginning, I started getting calls from ATV enthusiasts asking if they could ride their ATVs on the Jeep trails. When I checked into it, most trails allowed ATVs. So, as I updated the books, I started marking the ATV trails. Today, many ATVers swear by these books. They love the clear directions, photographs and simple maps.

In 2004, a Moab customer asked me if I would write an ATV book. This customer sold so many of my four-wheel-drive books to ATVers that he was sure an ATV book would be a big hit. I'd ridden an ATV a few times but didn't know too much about them. I decided to give it a try. Within a few months, I'd ridden over 1,600 miles and had enough information to write *ATV Trails Guide, Moab, UT*, which was published last year. The book has been very popular.

In the summer of 2006, I rode all the trails for this book, completing another 1,500 miles. So, with over 3,000 miles and two ATV books under my belt, I think I've learned a lot that will help you. If I've missed anything important that you think should have been included in this book, send an email to books@funtreks.com.

HOW TO USE THIS BOOK

Each trail in this book has a photo page, a general information page, a directions page and a map page. Read each page carefully before you head out.

The photo page is intended to show you actual trail conditions, not just scenery. Photos include both positive and negative aspects of a trail. A sample of the most difficult spot is usually included. Often photos make the trail look easier than it is. For example, photos of steep spots seldom look as steep as they really are.

The general information page provides directions to the start of the trail, where to unload and camp, difficulty details, highlights, time requirements, length of trail, a basic trail description, other routes nearby and services.

The directions page and map page work together as one. When the map is turned sideways, so are the directions. The two pages together can be copied (for personal use only) on one 8-1/2″ x 11″ sheet of paper and carried in your pocket while on the trail. The main route, described in the directions, is shown in green, blue or red depending on the difficulty level. This route has a shadow to help it stand out on the page. Other routes nearby are shown in light brown and are not described in the directions. Waypoints for the main route are shown on the directions page while waypoints for other routes are shown on the map. Mileage is shown with an overall grid. Check the scale at the bottom of the map because each scale is different. Directions were written from the author's personal notes and all maps were created using the author's own track logs.

THE RIGHT TRAIL FOR YOU

It is important to select a trail that matches your riding skills and your equipment. On page 9, you'll find a detailed description of each basic trail rating. Page 8 lists the trails in order of difficulty and the highest point of each trail. Within each category, trails are listed with easiest at the top and hardest at the bottom. Remember that ratings are subjective and can change quickly because of weather and other unforeseen circumstances.

If you are a novice rider, start with the easiest trails at the top of the list on page 8. After mastering basic skills, move down the list. The toughest trails at the bottom are for advanced riders only. Not everyone can attain this level. Don't let others pressure you into riding a trail beyond your skill level. Challenge yourself in small increments. Make sure you read each trail description yourself. Don't rely on others to translate.

ATVs come in all shapes, sizes and horsepower levels. Easy trails can generally be ridden with smaller 2-wheel-drive machines. As trails become more difficult, additional horsepower, 4-wheel drive and low-range gearing become more important. Steep rocky climbs require substantial horsepower. Small ATVs should not be used on steep, high elevation trails. These ATVs simply don't have enough horsepower to get the job done. If your ATV is underpowered for trails at sea level, it definitely won't cut it at 10,000 or 13,000 feet.

STAY ON THE TRAIL

There was a time in Colorado when getting from point A to point B required blazing a new trail across uncharted land. Pioneers who made these journeys were admired for their courage and determination. That was a long time ago. Colorado is a bit more populated these days. Our biggest problem now is people leaving existing trails and creating new ones. Despite everyone's best efforts to put a stop to this destructive behavior, it continues.

Unfortunately, a few thick-headed yahoos continue to spoil things for everybody. You know the type. They leave their trash for you to pick up, spray graffiti everywhere, use trail markers for target practice and, the worst sin of all, make new trails wherever they please. The result of this mindless behavior is trampled vegetation, needless erosion and ugly scars across our mountainsides. As a result, more and more trails are being closed to motorized recreation.

In my travels, I've talked to many forest/BLM rangers and land management people. Without exception, they all agree that the worst damage is coming from ATV and dirt bike use. Part of the problem is that many riders are kids and teenagers. Naturally rebellious, they don't understand the importance of following the rules. So, I ask all parents to educate their kids and keep them in check.

For the true offender, who knows what he's doing but just doesn't care, a warning: in Colorado, we don't take kindly to destruction of our beautiful state. Many Coloradans, if they see you committing a violation, will write down your registration number, take photos and report you to authorities. It's a crime to ride your ATV off the trail, crush vegetation, cause excessive noise, harass wildlife, vandalize property, remove historical artifacts and cause excessive pollution of air, land and water. The back country of Colorado is actively patrolled by National Forest and BLM rangers who take the above violations seriously. You will likely be required to pay a fine, appear in court or pay for damage. In worst cases, your ATV could be confiscated.

COLORADO OHV LAWS AND REGISTRATION REQUIREMENTS

Colorado residents: If you reside in Colorado, you must register your ATV and display numbered decals. Contact the Colorado State Parks Registration Unit at 13787 South Highway 85, Littleton, CO 80125, phone 303-791-1920. They can mail you an application or provide you with an address for the nearest walk-in outlet. Bring proof that you are the owner of the vehicle, which is usually a bill of sale. After you fill out the application and pay your registration fee ($15.25 in 2007), you will be issued a 60-day temporary permit that you must carry with you when riding until your decals arrive. At the time you receive your decals, you will also get your OHV registration card. You must carry this with you as well. All of this information is available online, including the application form, at www.parks.state.co.us. Once in the site, click on "Registrations."

When you purchase an ATV in Colorado, the dealer is required to collect the registration fee and send in the application. They will provide you with the 60-day temporary registration until your decals arrive. If you purchase an ATV from a private party, carry the dated bill of sale as a temporary registration. It's good for 30 days.

Out-of state residents: If you bring an OHV into Colorado from another state, you must have a registration from your home state. If your state does not have one, a Colorado non-resident OHV permit is required. These permits can be purchased anywhere Colorado hunting and fishing licenses are sold, or you can order online at www.parks. state.co.us. Once in the site, click on "Parks Store." ($15.25 in 2007.) Your home-state registration is good for 30 days. After that, you must purchase the same non-resident permit described above.

Unlicensed dirt bikes: Require same OHV registration as ATVs; however, rules for displaying the decals are slightly different.

Licensed, dual-purpose motorcycles: An OHV registration is not necessary since you already have a regular license and registration.

Exemptions: If you are using your ATV or dirt bike on your own property for non-commercial purposes or any private property with owner's permission, registration is not required. Certain organized events are sometimes given exemptions.

Required equipment: All ATVs must have working brakes, muffler and approved spark arrestor. Helmets and eye protection are not required by law, but are highly recommended.

ATV size recommedations by age: Follow manufacturers' recommendations for machine size relative to age as follows: 6 years old, 70ccs or smaller; 12 years old, between 70 and 90 ccs; 16 years old, 90ccs and larger. Riders should be tall enough to straddle their machines with both feet on the footrests with a slight bend at the knees. Young riders should be supervised by adults at all times. Dealers are bound by law to sell you a machine matched to your child's age.

Noise limits: The noise limit for vehicles in Colorado is 99 decibels. This is roughly equivalent to the loudness of a jack hammer or heavy truck. This decibel reading can be harmful to your hearing if experienced for a prolonged period of time.

Reporting accidents: You are required by law to report to local law enforcement any accident during which property damage exceeds $1,500 or when someone is hospitalized or killed.

Riding on public roads: OHVs cannot ride on public streets, roads or highways. In practice, this generally means paved roads and county roads used by normal, fast-moving, licensed traffic. Exceptions include crossing a road, crossing railroad tracks and crossing bridges. Questionable roads are often posted, but not always. Exceptions are allowed for declared emergencies.

ALTITUDE ADJUSTMENT OF CARBURETORS

If you have a fuel-injected engine, you can ignore this section. However, if your ATV has a carburetor, please read on.

Carburetors need to be properly jetted for Colorado's high altitude. The high points of each trail are shown on page 8. They range between

15

8,500 feet and 13,800 feet. Low points go down to about 6,000 feet. New ATVs are usually jetted to operate between 0 and 3,000 ft. Most people in Colorado have their machines jetted to operate between 6,000 and 9,000 feet and generally get by if they go higher. However, every machine is different and there is no guarantee your machine won't start to sputter at higher altitudes. Keep in mind that 19 trails in this book go above 10,000 feet.

Unfortunately, the problem can't be corrected by simply turning a set screw. The jet inside the carburetor must be changed. Unless you are a mechanic, you should take your machine to your local dealer. Colorado dealers are accustomed to dealing with this situation, so you may want to call ahead and make arrangements to have it done when you arrive. When you get home, you'll have to put the old jet back in.

Although I've never used one myself, I've been told about a product called "Dial-a-Jet," that once installed, allows the rider to adjust gas flow while on the trail. I've also been told that if you pop off your air box lid, you might gain another 1,000 feet in elevation. Just make sure no water gets inside while the lid is off.

NEW FOREST PLANS

All U.S. National Forests are in the process of executing a new plan that requires every forest in the United States to inventory all roads and reevaluate their use. All roads are subject to new designations and final designations will be communicated to the public in the form of a new type of map called an MVUM (Motor Vehicle Use Map). This project has been underway for some time. Some forests are near completion and others are years away. The Bureau of Land Management is doing something similar.

Motor Vehicle Use Maps. Unlike regular forest maps in color, MVUMs will be black and white. Only roads open to OHV use and a few access roads will appear on the maps. Closed roads will not appear. The maps will be free and readily available. They are designed in a simple way so that there will be less confusion as to which roads and trails are closed and which are open. If a road is not on the map, it is closed. Designation of the roads will not be dependent upon signage. In the past, because signs are often vandalized or removed, people have used this as an excuse to ride on a closed trail. This will no longer fly in the eyes of the law. With designation of the roads no longer in question, plans call for stronger, consistent enforcement.

What about the trails in this book? *Since final route designations are not complete as I write this book, I have no way to be sure all the trails shown here will be legal routes when the new plans are released.*

16

I've made every attempt to find out and, in some cases, I left out routes that had a higher probability of being closed. I'm fairly confident that most of the routes in this book will make the cut, but there is no way to know for sure. Therefore, it is up to you, the reader, to take this into consideration. The MVUM maps will supersede any information contained in this book. As soon as an MVUM becomes available, it is your responsibilty to verify that trails in this book are legal routes. If you are stopped by a law enforcement officer on a newly closed trail, showing him this book will not help a bit.

As information on trail closures becomes available to me, I will try, as quickly as possible, to post this information on my Web site at *www.funtreks.com*. If you know of something closed that is not posted, please send an email to *books@funtreks.com*.

IMPORTANT FACTS ABOUT COLORADO

When to ride. The length of the riding season in Colorado depends on the elevation of the trail and the amount of snow received over the winter. Some trails at low elevations open in late May. More trails open in June. High mountain passes typically can be crossed the first or second week in July. The best time of year to find most trails open is in August and September. September also is the peak time to enjoy the changing colors of the aspens. You may squeeze in some very late season riding in early October if no early winter snow has fallen. Hunting season starts in October.

The weather. Start as early as possible in the day. Mornings are usually clear while afternoons are often cloudy with a greater chance of thunderstorms. Colorado weather is often very pleasant and more moderate than people expect. Low humidity at high elevations keeps temperatures cool in the summer. In the winter, the sun shines most of the time and it stays relatively warm. There are few flies and mosquitoes except around wetlands. The downside to Colorado weather is that it is very unpredictable and can be extreme at times. Although it doesn't happen frequently, it can snow anytime during the summer, especially at higher elevations and at night when temperatures drop. Colorado can also be very windy. Pack plenty of warm clothing regardless of how hot it might be when you depart. Also, make sure you drink plenty of fluids to help you adapt to the dry thin air. Use sunscreen because you will sunburn quicker.

Lightning. Thunderstorms, hail, and lightning are very common in Colorado, especially in the late afternoon. Stay below timberline if you see a storm approaching. Lightning can strike from a distant storm even when it is sunny overhead.

Fires and floods. You must be aware of the possibility of forest fires and flash floods. Fires can move quickly, so watch for smoke when you are at higher points. At certain times of year, fire danger can be extremely high and the Forest Service will post fire danger warnings. During these times, campfires may be prohibited. Fines can be very steep for violators. Heavy rainstorms can cause flash floods at any time during the spring and summer. The danger is particularly acute if you are in a narrow canyon. If you have reason to believe a flash flood is imminent, do not try to outrun it. Abandon your vehicle and climb to higher ground.

Altitude sickness. Some people experience nausea, dizziness, headaches, or weakness the first time at high altitude. This condition usually improves over time. To minimize symptoms, give yourself time to acclimate, drink plenty of fluids, decrease salt intake, reduce alcohol and caffeine, eat foods high in carbohydrates and try not to exert yourself. If symptoms become severe, the only sure remedy is to return to a lower altitude. Consult your doctor if you have health problems.

Don't drink directly from streams or lakes. No matter how cool, clear or refreshing a mountain stream may appear, don't drink the water without boiling it, using a filter or iodine tablets. Although your chances of contracting Giardia are minimal, if you get it, it can be very serious. A friend of mine was very sick for nearly a year. The only exception would be a life-or-death situation.

SAFETY TIPS

Helmets. I speak from personal experience when I say wear a helmet. When I first started riding, I was thrown off my ATV against solid rock. My head and shoulder hit the rock with equal force. All the ligaments in my left shoulder were ripped apart, but because I was wearing a helmet, my head was fine. I am absolutely sure, had I not been wearing a helmet, I would have had some level of brain damage or perhaps been killed. The ironic thing about the accident was that I was hardly moving at the time. I tried to go up something steep and applied too much throttle. My ATV went straight up and I went flying backwards. You've seen it done many times on America's Funniest Videos and it looks pretty funny. But in real life, it can be deadly serious.

Colorado doesn't require adults or children to wear helmets, but officials will tell you it is extremely dangerous to ride without one. It doesn't take much of a knock on the head to permanently change your life. Allowing your child to ride without a helmet, in my opinion, is tantamount to child abuse.

Eye protection: You've probably felt debris hit your face when riding. It's inevitable that something will eventually hit you in the eye if you are not wearing protection. Why risk the pain and potential loss of sight? Always wear goggles or a face guard when you're moving.

Body protection. At minimum, wear gloves, long pants, a long-sleeve shirt and heavy leather boots. If possible, wear a chest protector to avoid being stabbed by a tree branch or other sharp object.

Speed control. Most accidents occur because of excessive speed. Be especially careful around blind curves. Don't follow too close. Leave your lights on all the time.

Emergencies. Figure out in advance what to do in an emergency.

Fuel limitations. Know how far your ATV will go on a tank of gas. Check your gas level frequently. If you carry extra gas, make sure it is in an approved container.

Riding at night. Avoid it whenever possible. Trails are difficult enough in the daylight. Allow plenty of time for your return trip. Always make sure your lights are working before you head out.

Stay together. Keep one another in sight to avoid getting split up. Make sure everyone knows the planned route. If you get separated and don't know what to do, wait along the planned route until your party finds you.

Carrying passengers. Unless your ATV is specifically designed for two people, don't carry a passenger. Many ATVs have room for a second person but are not really designed for it. A driver must be able to shift his weight quickly for balance. A second person on the back changes the weight ratio and restricts the driver's movements. This is particularly dangerous on Colorado's steep slopes. Many people, out of necessity, ride double, but it's not a good practice.

Be alert. Make sure you are well rested. It's a crime to ride while under the influence of alcohol or drugs.

Tell someone your plans. Always tell someone where you are going and when you plan to return. Leave a map of your route. Make sure you tell them when you return so they don't go out looking for you.

Travel with another vehicle. Walking out can be grueling and dangerous. In an emergency, a second vehicle could save a life.

Changing conditions. Colorado backcountry is fragile and under constant assault by forces of nature and man. Rock slides can occur or an entire road can be washed away overnight. A trail may be closed without notice. Be prepared to face unexpected situations.

Mines, tunnels and caves. Be careful around old mine buildings. Stay out of mines, tunnels and caves. They may look safe, but noxious gases may be present. Don't let children and pets play in these areas.

Safety Classes. Regardless of your level of experience, it's a good idea to take a safety class. If you buy a new ATV, you'll get a call from the ATV Safety Institute inviting you to one of their classes held locally across the country. Most manufacturers will pay you to attend. Ask your dealer about it.

TRIP PREPARATION

Think ahead. You probably can't prepare for every possible thing that can go wrong, but thinking about it ahead of time will improve your chances. Here are a few things to consider:

Vehicle readiness. Inspect and service your ATV regularly. Check belts, tires, battery, spark plug(s), fluids, lights, loose or worn parts. If you don't do your own wrenching, pay a qualified person to do it.

Know your ATV. It goes without saying, you must know how to operate your own ATV. If renting or borrowing equipment, make sure you are well instructed on its operation.

Check for trail closures. Call the BLM or Forest Service to find out if any trails are damaged or closed. Keep in mind, they may not be aware of damage if it occurred recently. (See contact information in appendix.)

Prepare for an overnight stay. It is not unusual to get stuck on a trail overnight. You'll rest easier if you are prepared.

Check the weather forecast. Weather can make or break your day. Read the section on Colorado's weather.

CHECKLIST OF EQUIPMENT AND SUPPLIES

It's daunting to list everything you might need on a trip. Where do you put it all? Try to miniaturize as much as possible. Check your ATV specifications for weight limits and distribute weight correctly front and rear. Everything should be securely tied down or in a carry box.
Basics:
   Plenty of water
   High-carbohydrate foods like energy bars
   Warm raincoat
   Small space blanket
   Small shovel
   Large trash bags (can be used for trash or rain protection)
   Map, compass (See map suggestions in this introduction.)
   Basic tool kit (My ATV came with a tiny tool kit.)
   Tow strap
   Waterproof matches and/or magnesium fire-starter
   Small flashlight (I like the tiny Maglite that doubles as a candle.)
   Small first aid kit and water purification tablets

Toilet paper, suncreen, insect repellent, pencil and paper
Knife or multi-purpose tool
Extra ignition key, prescription glasses, medications
Backup drive belt (need proper tools & knowledge to change)

Other things you may want:

Tire repair plug kit or can of tire sealant
CO2 cartridge gun or hand air pump (I carry an electric pump that plugs into 12-volt socket.)
Extra clothing, gloves, coat (or snowmobile suit in cold weather)
More complete set of tools (see suggestions below)
Larger first aid kit with instruction book
Small ice chest or insulated bag, larger choice of foods, drinks
Sleeping bag, small tent
Water purification filter
Large plastic tarp, nylon cords
Signal mirror, whistle, flare gun
Small set jumper cables
Extra gas, oil, fluids
Small fire extinguisher
Baling wire, duct tape, nylon zip ties and string
Extra spark plug(s)
Extra headlight bulb
Small assortment of nuts, bolts, clamps and cotter pins
Small axe or hatchet or folding saw
Cell phone (Regular cell phone is not reliable but take it anyway. Satellite phone is best if you can afford one.)
Small handheld CB radio or UHF radio
GPS unit with solid mount
Camera
Extra batteries
Winch or small come-along
Portable toilet (lightweight bag type) where required
Firewood (if camping where wood collection is prohibited)

Suggested tools:

Open end/box wrenches (check ATV for sizes)
Small socket set (check ATV for sizes)
Small adjustable wrench
Combination screwdriver with different tips
Spark plug wrench
Needle-nose pliers with wire cutter, Vise-Grips
Low pressure tire gauge

YOUR RESPONSIBILITIES AS A BACKCOUNTRY RIDER

Stay on existing routes. Leaving the trail causes unnecessary erosion, kills vegetation and spoils the beauty of the land. Scars remain for years. Don't widen the trail by riding around rocks and muddy spots. Don't take shortcuts or cut across switchbacks.

Wilderness areas and national parks. Boundaries for these areas are usually well marked. Riding inside these areas is a serious offense.

Stay off single-track trails. Nothing is more upsetting to a dirt biker or mountain biker than to have the trail widened by an ATV.

Private property. Some trails in this book are public roads that cross private property. These roads are usually well marked. As you pass through, you must stay on the road. You are trespassing anywhere else. Respect the rights of property owners. Pass through quietly, don't disturb livestock and leave gates the way you find them unless signs say otherwise.

Trash disposal. Carry bags and pack out your trash. Make an extra effort to pick up litter left by others.

Human waste. The disposal of human waste and toilet paper is becoming a big problem in the backcountry where facilities are not provided. Keep a small shovel handy and bury solid waste 6 to 12 inches deep, away from trails, campsites and at least 300 feet from any water source, which includes dry washes. Put toilet paper and hygiene products in a small plastic bag and dispose with trash. (Consider commercial Wag Bags. See at www.thepett.com.)

Noxious weeds. Thoroughly wash your ATV and transport vehicle between uses.

Camping. Generally, Forest Service and BLM camping guidelines allow dispersed camping along the trails. These spots are free and no services are provided. In some places, camping is restricted to designated sites. Here, you may find metal fire rings, toilets and sometimes picnic tables. Fees may be collected at self-service fee stations. Larger Forest Service campgrounds usually have more facilities and are located in the most popular areas.

When selecting a dispersed campsite along the trail, you can usually find a place where others have already camped. Often, rock fire rings have already been built. Do everything you can to avoid camping in a new spot. Rules for dispersed camping include a 14-day limit, packing out your trash, staying 100 feet away from water sources and not leaving campfires unattended. Always make sure your fire is dead out. Douse it thoroughly until it is cold to the touch. In addition, follow these low-impact camping techniques:

1. Don't burn cans, bottles, etc. in your campfire.

2. Use only dead and downed wood where collection is allowed.
3. Use a fire pan whenever possible. (This is a metal tray, like a garbage can lid, that holds ashes, which when cooled can be carried away with your trash.)
4. Heat water for cleaning rather than using soap.
5. If possible, use a propane stove for cooking. It's quick, easy and better for the environment.
6. Don't trample vegetation around the campsite. This causes the campsite to gradually enlarge until it becomes one huge bare area. And above all, don't let the kids ride their ATVs around the campsite.

COURTESY AND ETHICS

Riding an ATV in Colorado's backcountry is an experience you will remember for a lifetime. On many trails, you can ride for hours without seeing another person. The most popular trails, however, will be shared with hikers, bikers and horseback riders, most of whom are looking for quiet and solitude. Obviously, there is an inherent conflict when ATVs cross paths with non-motorized users.

When I'm on the trail, I do my best to mitigate the situation. I recognize that, although my ATV is quieter than most, it still makes noise and is going to irritate some people. I realize my riding kicks up dust and that, if I don't slow down, somebody is going to get upset. Since I hike and bike myself, it's easy to empathize with their situation. It's even more critical when animals are involved. I certainly don't want to run over anyone's dog or spook their horse.

The title "Courtesy and Ethics" suggests that the following actions are voluntary. In theory, that may be. In practice, however, following these suggestions is critical to the long-term survival of motorized recreation. Fair or not, OHV recreation has a tarnished image. We must all do our best to improve that image.

Overtaking hikers. Slow down well in advance to give time for your dust to settle. Swing wide and pass as slowly as possible. If they have a dog or pack animal, give them time to prepare. You may have to stop completely and shut off your engine. Every situation is different.

Oncoming hikers. On a wide road, move way over and go by as slowly as possible. On a narrower trail, pull over, shut off your engine and wait for them to walk by. Take off your helmet and exchange courtesies whenever possible. If they have a dog or pack animal, pull over sooner and stop until they are well past before starting your engine.

Overtaking horseback riders. This is the trickiest of all situations. You have to get close enough so they hear you, but not so close to spook the horses. Some horses stand quietly, others may bolt at the slightest provocation. You might have to stop, shut off your engine and walk toward the riders to discuss the situation. They may want to dismount or ride way off to the side.

Oncoming horseback riders. Pull over, as early as possible, shut off your engine and wait for them to pass. Take off your helmet and exchange greetings.

Mountain bikers. With slow-moving bikers, you handle the situation much the same as hikers. However, it gets more complicated when the bikers are riding fast. If you gradually catch up to them, you might want to slow down a bit and not pass at all. If you can't wait, make sure they know you are behind them, then go just fast enough to get by. You don't want to go too fast, but you don't want to dally beside them either. If bikers approach you from behind, just slow down and let them pass. A smile and a wave really help.

Making your ATV quieter. If you have a loud machine, ask your ATV dealer for suggestions to make it quieter. Make sure the muffler is working properly. Whatever you do, don't alter your existing muffler to make it louder.

Wildlife. It's a crime to harass wild animals. Deer are the most frequent critters you'll see, but many other animals abound. Most scurry off before you know they're there, but sometimes you get lucky and they hang around long enough to snap a picture. Almost every time I go into the high mountains in the Radical Hill area, I've seen mountain goats up close while moving slowly on my ATV.

Carry extra water for others: This is a personal thing that I like to do. I've been able to help some desperate people over the years.

CARRY EXTRA MAPS

Before you go anywhere, make sure you have a good topographic map of the area. The maps in this book will clearly direct you along the trail; however, if you get lost or decide to venture down a side road, you'll need more detail.

National Forest maps are the most commonly used. More than one map may be necessary if the trail crosses forest boundaries. Forest Service maps are usually the least expensive but are not frequently updated. The Forest Service is working on new improved maps that will compare to the best maps out there.

I like *Latitude 40°* maps and *Trails Illustrated Maps by National Geographic*. These maps are updated frequently and are made of durable waterproof plastic. They include topographic information and the graphics are superb. The maps cover a smaller area, so you may need more of them. Newer *Latitude 40°* maps differentiate Jeep trails, ATV trails and single-track routes. Their map of the Crested Butte/Taylor Park area is absolutely a must purchase if you ride there.

A map book I strongly recommend is *DeLorme's Colorado Atlas & Gazetteer*. It covers the entire state in great detail. If you look closely, you can find most of the backroads in this book. Although it is a bit bulky to carry on an ATV, I go through the trouble of fitting it in somewhere. Sometimes I end up in places I didn't expect. As long as I have this atlas, I can always find my way home.

Today, many people are using mapping software on their computers and printing their own maps. GPS units are becoming more sophisticated. Built-in software is getting quite detailed. On some units you can upload very detailed maps covering a smaller area.

Whatever you use, spend time looking over the maps before you head out. Familiarize yourself as much as possible with the area. When you get on the trail, don't be surprised to find inaccuracies. Signs don't always match the map.

Other route-finding tips. Make sure you are familiar with BLM and Forest Service trail markers. Understanding what they mean can make a difference. However, don't depend on them. They are often removed or vandalized. Keep track of your mileage; don't guess. If you don't have an odometer, use a GPS unit for mileage.

GLOBAL POSITIONING

Consider buying a GPS unit if you haven't done so already. Prices have really come down and they've become quite simple to use. The unit doesn't have to be fancy, just good enough to provide accurate coordinates. When used with *DeLorme's Atlas*, you can easily figure out where you are. More expensive GPS units have built-in maps and allow you to download and upload information into your computer. You would probably like these features, too, but they are not necessary.

I used GPS while working on this book. Frankly, I've found it to be an indispensable tool. I didn't know how well my unit *(Garmin GPS V)* would work outside with the jarring and inclement weather, but it worked flawlessly. I bought a great mount *(RAM-B-149Z-GA2)* that held it firmly in place on my handlebars. I plug the power cord into my 12-volt power socket and I never worry about batteries. At the end of the day, I download my tracklog and waypoints into the computer and print out my entire route. (See appendix for contact information on GPS companies.)

GPS Settings. All the trails in this book show key GPS waypoints in Latitude/Longitude format in hours/minutes.hundredths of minutes. Don't confuse this format with hours/minutes/seconds which looks similar. Make sure your GPS unit displays in the same format or your readings will appear in error. Set your Datum for WGS 84 or NAD83 (not NAD27).

BACKCOUNTRY SURVIVAL

Self-reliance. Most of us live in populated areas and are accustomed to having other people around when things go wrong. In Colorado's remote backcountry, you must be self-reliant. Don't count on anyone else's help.

Basic tips. Pack high-carbohydrate energy foods and plenty of warm clothing. Carry and drink plenty of water; don't wait until you get thirsty. Build a shelter, collect firewood and build a fire before dark. Know how to build a smoky fire with wet leaves so a search party can find you. Carry a whistle or signal mirror. Read a book on survival. Watch *Survivorman* on TV (not the same as *Survivor*).

Make sure you can start a fire. The easiest tool for starting a fire is waterproof matches. But I also carry a magnesium/flint block for extra insurance. But learn how to use it. You have to shave off filings from the magnesium and make a little pile. When you strike the flint side and make a spark, the magnesium bursts into a very hot flame that usually works even in the rain. This device is sold at any good camping store.

Keep yourself dry, prevent hypothermia. Make sure you have adequate rain gear. Dress in layers. Wool is best because it keeps you warm even when it's wet. Don't overwork and sweat under your clothing. Dampness leads to hypothermia, which is your biggest enemy. If your core body temperature drops only slightly, your body can shut down in a gradual way that is not apparent to you. The best way to deal with hypothermia is to prevent it in the first place.

First Aid. Always carry a good first-aid kit. Take a first-aid course and learn the basics. Make sure the kit contains first-aid instructions.

What to do if you have mechanical problems or you get lost. Stay with your ATV. There's always a chance that someone will come along if you stay near the road. Your ATV is easier to see than you are. If you get lost or separated from your group, stay in one place. If you're familiar with the area and know exactly how far it is to hike out, consider walking out.

If you have a cell phone, try to find a high point where you can get a signal and call for help. Although your chances are slim that your phone will work in Colorado's remote backcountry, there's always a chance. If you have a medical emergency, call 911. If you can afford a satellite phone, get one.

OHV ORGANIZATIONS AND CAMPAIGNS

COHVCO (Colorado Off Highway Vehicle Coalition). This is the most active OHV organization in Colorado. In addition to an extensive education program, they spend a great deal of money fighting legislation aimed at closing ATV, dirt bike and Jeep trails in the state of Colorado. If you want to help in the fight to keep your local trails open, there is no better way than to support this organization.

"Stay the Trail" Program. This highly recognized campaign is a joint venture of COHVCO and Colorado State Parks OHV Registration Program. The mission of the program is to reinforce responsible OHV use in an effort to minimize resource damage on public land. The program has made great strides and is quickly gaining the support of the U.S. Forest Service and other land management agencies.

ATVA. (All-Terrain Vehicle Association.) Joining this national organization can help you get more fun out of your ATV. Your membership dues, in part, are used to fight anti-OHV legislation. ATVA's motto is "United we stand. Divided we're banned."

Colorado ATV clubs. The following ATV clubs have been very active in their support and promotion of responsible ATV use in Colorado: Colorado Quad Runners, Thunder Mountain Wheelers, Royal Gorge ATV Club, High Rocky Riders Off Road Club and the Western Slope ATV Association.

BlueRibbon Coalition. This national organization's motto is "Preserving Our Natural Resouces FOR the Public Instead of FROM the Public." No group fights harder on a national basis for motorized recreation. Join today and start receiving their informative BlueRibbon Magazine.

United Four Wheel Drive Association and Colorado Association of 4-Wheel Drive Clubs. Their titles say "four wheel drive," but both of these organizations have a huge impact on ATV and dirt bike trails.

To join or support any of these organizations, see appendix for contact information.

FINAL COMMENTS

I've made every effort to make this book as accurate and as easy to use as possible. If you have ideas for improvements or find any significant errors, please write to me at FunTreks, Inc., P.O. Box 3127, Monument, CO 80132-3127. Or e-mail to *books@funtreks.com*. Whether you're a novice or experienced rider, I hope this book makes your backcountry experience safer, easier and more fun.

Map Legend

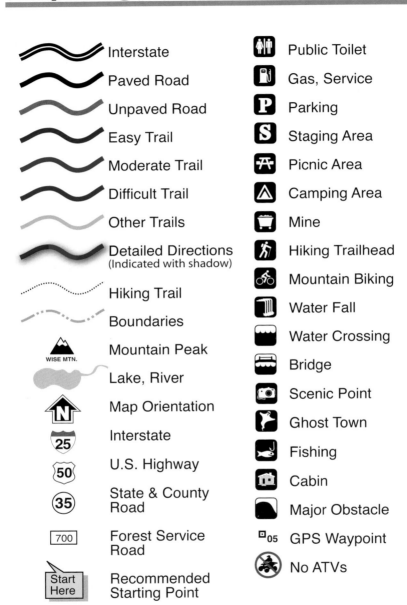

Interstate

Paved Road

Unpaved Road

Easy Trail

Moderate Trail

Difficult Trail

Other Trails

Detailed Directions
(Indicated with shadow)

Hiking Trail

Boundaries

Mountain Peak
WISE MTN.

Lake, River

Map Orientation

Interstate
25

U.S. Highway
50

State & County
Road
35

Forest Service
Road
700

Recommended
Starting Point
Start
Here

Public Toilet

Gas, Service

Parking

Staging Area

Picnic Area

Camping Area

Mine

Hiking Trailhead

Mountain Biking

Water Fall

Water Crossing

Bridge

Scenic Point

Ghost Town

Fishing

Cabin

Major Obstacle

GPS Waypoint

No ATVs

THE TRAILS

Fun section on North Divide 717 OHV Area, Trail #24.

Starting point. Staging areas have modern vault toilets and plenty of room to park.

One of many dispersed camping spots.

Steep slopes around perimeter of dunes.

Dunes surrounded by snow-capped mountains in fall.

Fun trails north of dunes.

Getting There: About 115 miles northwest of Fort Collins—allow about 2-1/2 hours. A very long drive but the scenery is superb. A good weekend outing. From Fort Collins, head west on Highways 14 & 287 following signs to Laramie. At Ted's Place, bear left on Highway 14 towards Walden. Turn right at gas stations in Walden on Highway 125 and go another 10 miles north to Cowdrey. About a mile north of Cowdrey, turn right on C.R. 6. Head east 3.3 miles and bear right on BLM Road 2509. After another 1.5 miles, bear left to main camping area. (Right here goes to alternate starting point nearer the dunes.)

Staging/Camping: Plenty of dispersed camping within walking distance of toilets. Road is sandy and soft in places. Inspect firmness of area when selecting a camp spot.
(Website: www.co.blm.gov/kra/NorthSandHillSRMA.htm)

Difficulty: The introductory loop described here is easy. However, steep slopes around perimeter of dunes can be very difficult. Dirt roads north of dunes are narrow, steep and difficult in places.

Highlights: Unique opportunity to ride on sand dunes in Colorado. Area is small but a great deal of fun. Explore a network of dirt roads north of the dunes. Stay on existing roads at all times. Whip flags and helmets are recommended. Bring your own firewood. Pack out trash.

Time & Distance: Introductory loop described here is about 7.2 miles and takes about an hour. Allow a day to explore the entire area.

Trail Description: First part of loop follows sandy road through aspen trees. Many tight turns and whoops. Climb to dunes and follow perimeter clockwise. South of dunes, head west on more defined roads, then northwest back to 2509. East on 2509 goes back to start.

Other Nearby Routes: As you wind through Poudre Canyon along Highway 14, you'll pass several OHV routes not covered in this book, including Kelly Flats, Green Ridge and Baker Pass. Colorado State Forest State Park also has some fun routes. These trails are described in *Guide to Northern Colorado Backroads & 4-Wheel Drive Trails.*

Services: Basic services, gas and convenience stores in Walden.

Directions: (Shadowed portion of trail is described here.)

WP	Mile	Action
01	0.0	N40° 52.62′ W106° 12.56′ Continue under power lines past Toilet #1. Stay slightly left on defined road as it drops downhill.
02	0.1	N40° 52.66′ W106° 12.48′ Stay right. Left goes to North Sand Dunes Road and network of fun roads on state land.
03	0.7	N40° 52.52 W106° 11.95′ Turn right uphill to Harvey's Hill (marked with red post) before road ends at loop. Climb hill to dunes.
	0.8	Stay left following perimeter of dunes as you gradually swing south. Many steep roads drop off edge of dunes into aspen groves.
04	2.0	N40° 52.33 W106° 11.66′ Follow fence line southwest along valley between dunes. Bear left across valley at convenient point. Again, bear left around perimeter of dunes.
	3.5	As you reach southern end of dunes, start heading west. As you come out of dunes into more sagebrush, a road will form.

WP	Mile	Action
05	4.1	N40° 51.76 W106° 12.05′ Bear right away from fence line at fork.
	4.4	Pass through opening in fence where roads converge. Continue a short distance to better road.
06	4.5	N40° 51.99 W106° 12.38′ Turn right on better road to reach alternate starting point at base of dunes by Toilet #3.
07	4.9/0.0	N40° 52.20 W106° 12.11′ Turn around and return to Waypoint 06. Then bear right heading northwest on wide graded road.
08	1.4	N40° 52.44′ W106° 13.37′ After passing under power lines, turn right on Road #2509 (where you originally came in).
09	1.8	N40° 52.62′ W106° 13.05′ Continue straight. Road to left goes to more camping and Toilet #2.
01	2.3	Arrive back at starting point.

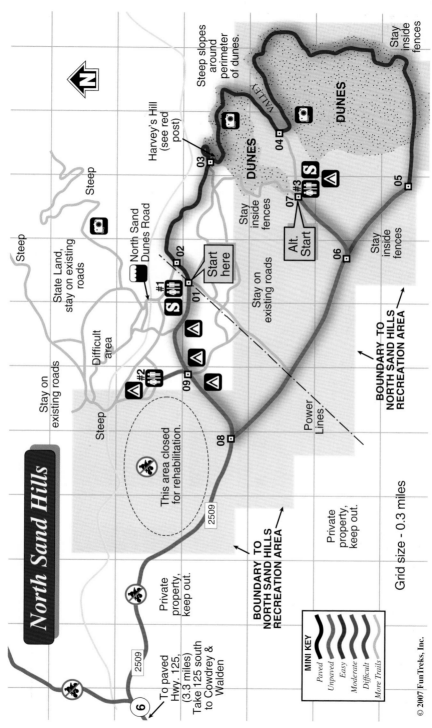

North Sand Hills

Steep slopes around perimeter of dunes.

Stay inside fences

Harvey's Hill (see red post)

DUNES

DUNES

VALLEY

Steep

Steep

Steep

State Land, stay on existing roads

North Sand Dunes Road

Stay on existing roads

Stay inside fences

Difficult area

Stay inside fences

Stay on existing roads

Alt. Start

Start here

Stay inside fences

Power Lines

BOUNDARY TO NORTH SAND HILLS RECREATION AREA

Stay on existing roads

Steep

This area closed for rehabilitation.

BOUNDARY TO NORTH SAND HILLS RECREATION AREA

Private property, keep out.

Private property, keep out.

Grid size - 0.3 miles

To paved Hwy. 125, (3.3 miles) Take 125 south to Cowdrey & Walden

MINI KEY	
Paved	
Unpaved	
Easy	
Moderate	
Difficult	
More Trails	

© 2007 FunTreks, Inc.

01 02 03 04 05 06 07 08 09

#1 #2 #3

2509

6

33

Start of trail has seasonal gate.

No camping at staging area.

Tough spot at half-mile point.

Twisting route is fun to ride.

Proceed cautiously. Don't take unnecessary risks.

One of many camp spots.

Moody Hill

Getting There: **From Loveland** take Hwy. 34 west and turn right on Hwy. 27 towards Masonville. Turn left at Masonville and continue another 10.7 miles to Buckhorn Road 44H on left. Go west 1.5 miles to F.S. 513 on left. **From Ft. Collins:** Take Hwy. 14 bypass through LaPorte and follow Rist Canyon Road west to Stove Prairie Road 27. Turn left and go 4 miles south to Buckhorn Rd. 44H on right.

Staging/Camping: Large parking area across road at entrance to trail (no camping here). Plenty of dispersed camping along route. Camp in existing spots with stone fire rings as much as possible

Difficulty: For advanced riders only. The first half mile is very steep and rocky. The middle portion varies between easy and moderate. The last 1.7 miles is very steep with ledges and loose rock.

Highlights: Challenging forest ride close to Loveland and Ft. Collins. Scenery is pleasant but not outstanding. Primitive camping along route but no developed campgrounds.

Time & Distance: As described here, one-way trip to top is about 9 miles. Allow 3 to 4 hours for round trip depending upon riding skills. Add time to explore side roads.

Trail Description: Trail begins with challenging climb then levels out along F.S. 132. Final climb to top of Crystal Mountain may be too difficult for all but the most daring riders. Side roads are short and mainly lead to camp spots. Stay on marked forest roads at all times. Violations could result in this area being permanently closed to OHV use. Pack out your trash.

Other Nearby Routes: Storm Mountain, Trail # 3. Not covered in this book are: Ballard Road (F.S. 154) and West White Pine Mountain Road (F.S. 100), located another 8 to 9 miles west on Buckhorn Road. ATVs are not allowed on Buckhorn Road 44H.

Services: Gas and restaurant at Vern's Place in LaPorte west of Fort Collins. Masonville Mercantile is an interesting stop if coming from Loveland. Commercial RV campgrounds along Hwy. 34 west of Loveland. Rocky Mountain National Park not far away.

Directions: *(Shadowed portion of trail is described here.)*

WP	Mile	Action
01	**0.0**	*N40° 34.26´ W105° 20.87´* From staging area, cross Buckhorn Road and begin steep climb up F.S. 513.
	0.5	Steepest, rockiest spot on lower part of trail. Be very careful not to flip backwards.
	1.1	Continue straight where 513A goes right. This is a short spur to camp spots.
	1.7	Continue straight. Road on left dead ends at camp spot with so-so view.
02	**2.6/0.0**	*N40° 33.81 W105° 22.96´* Reach top of hill at F.S. 132. Right dead ends at stone quarry in another 0.7 miles. F.S. 513C, near top of hill, dead ends after 0.4 miles. After side trips, reset odometer and continue southwest on 132.
	0.3	Bear left. F.S. 132B goes right to large camp spots and loop with overlook.
	1.5	Rocky stretch improves after seasonal gate.

WP	Mile	Action
	2.4	Continue straight. F.S. 132D goes right. (Not much to see on this side trip.)
03	**2.5**	*N40° 32.73 W105° 24.79´* Major intersection. Don't go right or left on private roads. Continue straight on F.S. 344. Road turns south and is mildly rough in spots. More camp spots along the way.
04	**4.0**	*N40° 31.99 W105° 24.48´* Stay right downhill as you intersect with better road.
	4.3	Bear right.
05	**4.6**	*N40° 31.71´ W105° 24.78´* Bear right again and immediately encounter first obstacle. This starts difficult climb to Crystal Mountain.
06	**6.5**	*N40° 32.23´ W105° 26.03´* Primary trail ends near top of mountain above 9700 feet elevation. Some views. Turn around and return the way you came.

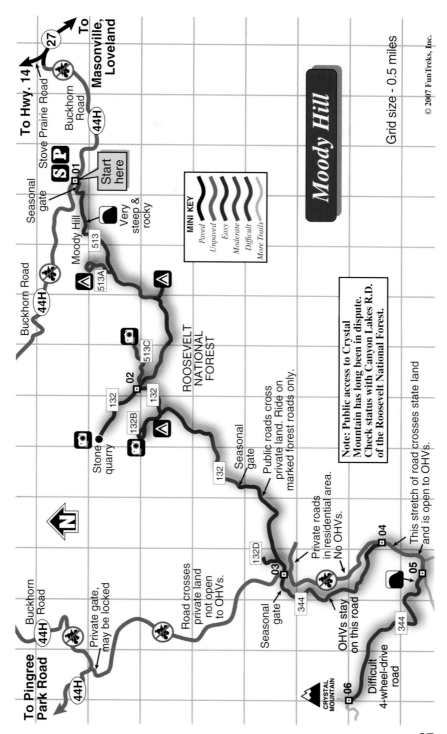

To Hwy. 14

27 To Masonville, Loveland

Stove Prairie Road

SP

Buckhorn Road

44H

Seasonal gate

Start here

01

Moody Hill

513

Very steep & rocky

513A

Buckhorn Road

44H

513C

02

132

132

132B

Stone quarry

ROOSEVELT NATIONAL FOREST

132

Seasonal gate

Public roads cross private land. Ride on marked forest roads only.

MINI KEY

Paved
Unpaved
Easy
Moderate
Difficult
More Trails

Moody Hill

Grid size - 0.5 miles

© 2007 FunTreks, Inc.

To Pingree Park Road

44H

Buckhorn Road

44H

Private gate, may be locked

Road crosses private land not open to OHVs.

132D

Seasonal gate

03

344

Private roads in residential area. No OHVs.

OHVs stay on this road

04

05

This stretch of road crosses state land and is open to OHVs.

344

Difficult 4-wheel-drive road

CRYSTAL MOUNTAIN

06

Note: Public access to Crystal Mountain has long been in dispute. Check status with Canyon Lakes R.D. of the Roosevelt National Forest.

N

37

Most of route is easy to moderate.

Steep challenge leaving Galuchie Meadow.   Locked gate at east end of F.S. 153.

Looking east towards front range from top of 9,918-ft. Storm Mountain.

Storm Mountain

Getting There: From Loveland, head west on Highway 34 about 16 miles. Just after Drake, turn right on C.R. 43. Go 0.2 miles and turn right across bridge. Climb steep road to Cedar Park residential area. After 2 miles, turn left at T, then follow signs for Storm Mountain Road, F.S. 128. Road climbs through burn area to forest gate at 6.6 miles. No unlicensed vehicles allowed until you get inside gate.

Staging/Camping: Just a few places to park and camp inside gate. More room is available just ahead at Galuchie Meadow. Many dispersed camp spots along route.

Difficulty: Difficult rating comes from one unavoidable steep section west of Galuchie Meadow (see photo at left). Most roads are easy to moderate, except for optional 153C, which is very steep in places.

Highlights: Great views of front range from Storm Mountain near 10,000 ft. Eastern end of F.S.153 passes through recovering burn area. Locked gate (except during hunting season) at eastern end of 153 stops you about 1.5 miles before Stove Prairie Road. Crossing private property beyond closed gate can result in $1,000 fine and/or one year in prison. All other roads dead end at gates to private property.

Time & Distance: Over 20 miles of roads (you'll cover over 40 miles if you ride everything described here). Storm Mountain can be reached quickly in less than an hour. Allow a full day for everything.

Trail Description: The climb to Storm Mountain is very steep but the views are worth the effort. F.S. 153B has a scenic rock outcrop but not much to see after that. F.S. 153C descends steeply and gradually narrows to a hiking trail. The long ride east through the burn area is desolate but the terrain is fun. There's an unmarked primitive camping area (no toilet) at Nelson Spring. (If there was a natural spring in the area, I couldn't find it.). The ride beyond Nelson Spring on F.S. 345 was pleasant but uneventful. (I didn't ride F.S. 345B.)

Services: Full services in Loveland and Estes Park. Several commercial RV campgrounds along Highway 34. No gas in Drake. Estes Park and Rocky Mountain National Park are another 10 to 12 miles west of Drake on Highway 34.

Directions: *(Shadowed portion of trail is described here.)*

WP	Mile	Action
02	**0.0**	Reset odometer and continue east on 153 past Galuchie Meadow. Fun ride follows as trail undulates along varied terrain through Bear Gulch.
05	**3.7**	N40° 30.04′ W105° 19.79′ **Left** on 345 goes to Nelson Spring. After steep switchbacks, 345 passes a wide camping spot then levels out, eventually ending in another 4.3 miles. (On way, stay right where 345B goes left.) **Right** at Waypoint 05 continues through burn area another 4.5 miles to locked gate. (On way, stay left on 153 when 348 goes right to Spruce Mountain.)
06	**8.2**	N40° 30.47′ W105° 15.83′ Locked gate (except during hunting season). Turn around and retrace route back to start.

WP	Mile	Action
01	**0.0**	N40° 28.54′ W105° 22.30′ Pass through gate and look for wide spot to park. More space is available just ahead at Galuchie Meadow.
02	**0.1**	N40° 28.66′ W105° 22.38′ Turn left at Galuchie Meadow.
	0.4	Enter forest and climb steeply through toughest part of trail.
03	1.7	N40° 29.06′ W105° 23.53′ Stay right and climb steep meadow. At top of meadow, trail swings right across face of mountain through trees.
04	2.4	N40° 29.10 W105° 23.11′ Main route ends at view point. Turn around and return to Waypoint 03.
03	3.1	Bear right on 153. Trail soon splits. 153B goes right past rock outcrop and ends after another 3 miles. 153C drops steeply downhill to left and eventually dwindles to hiking trail. Return to Waypoint 02.

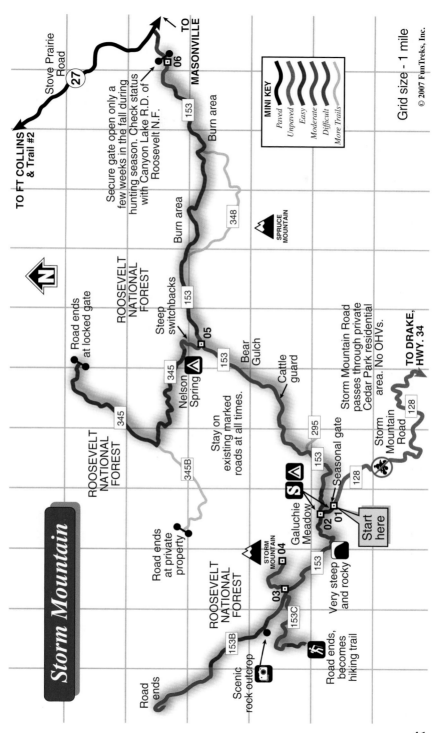

Storm Mountain

TO FT COLLINS
& Trail #2

Stove Prairie Road

27

TO MASONVILLE

Secure gate open only a few weeks in the fall during hunting season. Check status with Canyon Lake R.D. of Roosevelt N.F.

06

153

Burn area

Burn area

348

SPRUCE MOUNTAIN

MINI KEY

Paved
Unpaved
Easy
Moderate
Difficult
More Trails

Grid size - 1 mile

© 2007 FunTreks, Inc.

N

ROOSEVELT NATIONAL FOREST

Road ends at locked gate

Steep switchbacks

153

05

153

Bear Gulch

Cattle guard

Nelson Spring

345

Stay on existing marked roads at all times.

345

345B

ROOSEVELT NATIONAL FOREST

Road ends at private property

295

153

Seasonal gate

128

Storm Mountain Road passes through private Cedar Park residential area. No OHVs.

TO DRAKE, HWY. 34

128

Storm Mountain Road

01

Start here

S

Galuchie Meadow

02

153

Very steep and rocky

STORM MOUNTAIN

04

03

153C

153B

ROOSEVELT NATIONAL FOREST

Scenic rock outcrop

Road ends, becomes hiking trail

Road ends

Road ends

Dramatic view from the "Notch."

Twisting roads are fun to ride.

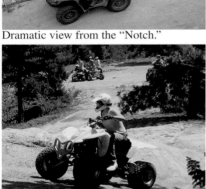

Great family-fun area.

One of several scenic camp spots.

Easy way up is on left side; right side is difficult—your choice!

Pole Hill 4

Getting There: **From Estes Park:** Take Hwy. 36 east past Lake Estes. A short distance before mile marker 4, turn left on Pole Hill Road, C.R. 122. Follow wide gravel road uphill through Meadowdale Hills residential area and turn left at 0.8 miles on F.S. 122. **From Boulder:** Take Highway 36 northwest about 35 miles. Before you get to Estes Park, turn right on Pole Hill Road, C.R. 122, about 0.2 miles after mile marker 4. Follow wide gravel road uphill 0.8 miles through Meadowdale Hills residential area and turn left on F.S. 122.

Staging/Camping: Parking is limited at trailhead. Don't park on residential street. If necessary, drive in a short distance on F.S. 122 and park at wide spot, but don't block road. No camping at start of trail, but you'll find plenty of dispersed camping along route. The first part of F.S.122 is steep and rocky and requires 4-wheel drive. Obey all signs.

Difficulty: Easy to moderately challenging with intermittent rocky climbs. Difficult spots can be bypassed.

Highlights: A small area but the riding is fun. Great place to camp with family over a weekend but you'll have to carry camping gear on ATV. Confined area limits kids wandering off too far. Make sure everyone stays on marked trails at all times. Don't trample vegetation around campsites. Don't cut across meadows or shortcut between roads.

Time & Distance: Loop route described here is about 6 miles. Allow about an hour for initial tour of area, then ride loops in different directions exploring other roads you missed the first time.

Trail Description: Entry to area under power lines is very rocky and steep in places. F.S. 247C climbs very steep hill then loops back through trees. F.S. 122A is narrow for Jeeps but perfect for ATVs.

Other Activities: Estes Park is a popular tourist town and serves as the eastern gateway to Rocky Mountain National Park. Main Street is flooded with tourists in the summer. The town offers all kinds of fun outdoor activities including outstanding hiking trails.

Services: Full services in Estes Park including many commercial campgrounds. No services or toilets along trail.

Directions: *(Shadowed portion of trail is described here.)*

WP	Mile	Action
01	0.0	*N40° 21.71′ W105° 26.94′* Head east past seasonal gate. Pole Hill Road 122 follows power lines uphill on steepest, rockiest part of trail.
	0.4	Optional road to left goes to terrific scenic camp spot.
	0.7	Stay left. Alternate 247A goes right.
02	0.8	*N40° 21.64′ W105° 26.09′* At 4-way intersection, turn right and climb 247.
03	1.7	*N40° 21.44 W105° 25.23′* Turn left downhill on 247C. Pass road on left, cross meadow and climb steep hill. Follow loop clockwise through trees back downhill.
	2.4	Turn right on 247. Road to left is gated and is hiking only to Panorama Peak.
	2.8	Stay right. Left is alternate 247A.
03	3.0	Back to Waypoint 03 again. Turn right on 247C, only this time, when you get to bottom of hill before meadow, turn left. Follow road downhill through trees.

WP	Mile	Action
04	3.7	*N40° 21.84′ W105° 25.64′* At T intersection, turn right.
	3.8	Bear left on lesser 122A. Road to right dead ends at gate at top of steep hill.
05	4.6	*N40° 22.22 W105° 26.04′* Turn right on well defined road to great camp spot. Nearby rock outcrop has stunning views. Don't turn too soon, or you'll miss the best spot.
	5.0	After visiting camp spot, continue counterclockwise around loop to the "Notch." This is a great photo spot from rock outcrop on left above road.
	5.5	Stay right. (Left repeats loop you've just done.) You are now back on F.S 122 which soon connects to the road on which you entered.
02	6.0	Back to 4-way intersection. Straight goes back to start of trail or continue to explore other roads you missed the first time.

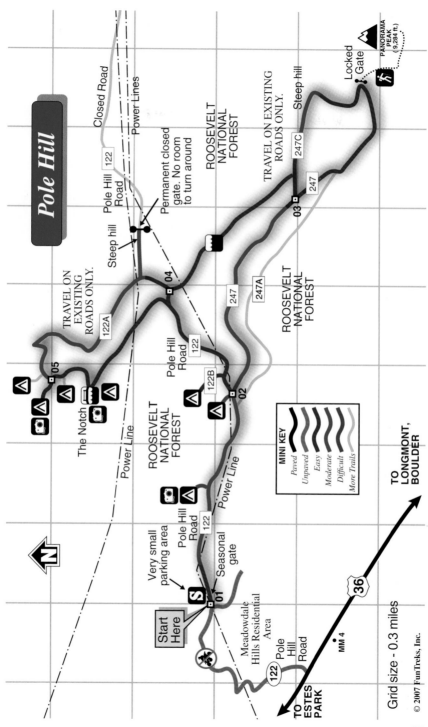

Pole Hill

Closed Road

Power Lines

PANORAMA PEAK (9,284 ft.)

Locked Gate

Steep hill

ROOSEVELT NATIONAL FOREST

TRAVEL ON EXISTING ROADS ONLY.

247C

247

03

Pole Hill Road   122

Permanent closed gate. No room to turn around

Steep hill

04

TRAVEL ON EXISTING ROADS ONLY.

122A

247

247A

ROOSEVELT NATIONAL FOREST

05

Pole Hill Road   122

122B

02

The Notch

Power Line

ROOSEVELT NATIONAL FOREST

MINI KEY
Paved
Unpaved
Easy
Moderate
Difficult
More Trails

TO LONGMONT, BOULDER

N

Power Line

Pole Hill Road   122

Very small parking area

Seasonal gate

Meadowdale Hills Residential Area

S

01

Start Here

122   Pole Hill Road

36

MM 4

TO ESTES PARK

Grid size - 0.3 miles

© 2007 FunTreks, Inc.

45

Unload at the Idleglen staging area at start of Stillwater Pass Road 123.

Stillwater Pass Road couldn't be easier.

Kawuneeche Road in the fall.

Trees open up along route to expose great views of lakes below.

Stillwater Pass Road follows picturesque Willow Creek on western side.

Stillwater Pass Road ⑤

Getting There: From Highway 34 south of Grand Lake (0.3 miles south of mile marker 10 across from Dilly Docks), take County Road 4 northwest. This road starts paved, then changes to gravel. After 3 miles, bear left on Stillwater Pass Road 123. (Staging area is just ahead.) Kawuneeche Road 120 is to the right.

Staging/Camping: You'll park in the large staging area that services the trail system for the Idleglen OHV Area, Trail #6. If camping, continue past the staging area to numerous dispersed camping spots along Stillwater Pass Road and marked side roads. This is a very popular area on summer weekends, so arrive early to get the best camp spots.

Difficulty: The easiest route in this book. Well-graded gravel all the way. You share the road with licensed vehicles, dirt bikes and mountain bikes, so ride defensively and watch your speed.

Highlights: Great ride for beginners. As you cruise along, note entry and exit points of Idleglen OHV trails that crisscross the main road. For details of these routes see Trail #6.

Time & Distance: Stillwater Pass Road is 20 miles one way. Kawuneeche Road is 9 miles one way. If you ride both routes out and back, you will have covered about 58 miles. Allow at least a half day.

Trail Description: Scenic views at various points along the route. Stillwater Pass is not marked. You probably won't be aware that you are crossing the pass unless you keep track of your altitude. West side of pass has gentle grades as road follows alongside picturesque Willow Creek much of the way. Three 4x4 routes shown on map offer a bit more challenge than the main road, but these routes are not as difficult as the narrower Idleglen ATV trails. Kawuneeche Road has great fall color. Roads are generally open June 1 through November 15.

Services: Modern vault toilet at Idleglen staging area. Gas at general store on corner of Highway 34 and West Portal Road. Many services in town of Grand Lake.

Special Map: Arapaho National Forest OFF-HIGHWAY VEHICLE MAP of Stillwater Pass Area. Contact Sulphur Ranger District.

Directions: *(Shadowed portion of trail is described here.)*

WP	Mile	Action
01	**0.0**	*N40° 13.54´ W105° 53.55´* From Idleglen staging area near start of Stillwater Pass Road 123, head west. You'll see many excellent dispersed camping spots along the road within the first few miles. More spots can be found on marked side roads.
	3.1	The trees thin out allowing dramatic views of lakes below.
	5.5	Continue straight. F.S. 190 goes left. This road climbs to a network of smaller roads with great views.
02	**5.6/0.0**	*N40° 14.93´ W105° 57.52´* F.S. 816.1, Little Gravel Mountain 4x4 Spur Road goes left. This moderate 3-mile loop goes uphill then circles west and connects to F.S. 190, which brings you back to 123.
	2.2	Stay right on 123 where road goes left to Gravel Mountain. F.S. 123 soon narrows to one lane.

WP	Mile	Action
03	**3.5**	*N40° 16.66´ W105° 58.57´* Stay right on main road again. Gravel Mountain loop 815.2 rejoins 123 on left. You are near highest point of route, over 10,700 ft.
04	**8.4**	*N40° 18.70´ W105° 58.65´* After long downhill stretch, continue straight where Lost Lake Road 123.3 joins on right.
05	**14.2/0.0**	*N40° 18.56´ W106° 03.78´* More side roads follow as you gradually descend along Willow Creek to Hwy. 125. Turn around at parking area before Hwy. 125.
01	**14.2/0.0**	Return to staging area. To ride Kawuneeche Road, continue past staging area and turn left at next major intersection onto F.S. 120.
06	**9.0**	*N40° 17.89´ W105° 54.67´* Very easy road ends at parking lot for hiking trail. Towards the end, you'll pass 4x4 roads for North and South Supply Creek.

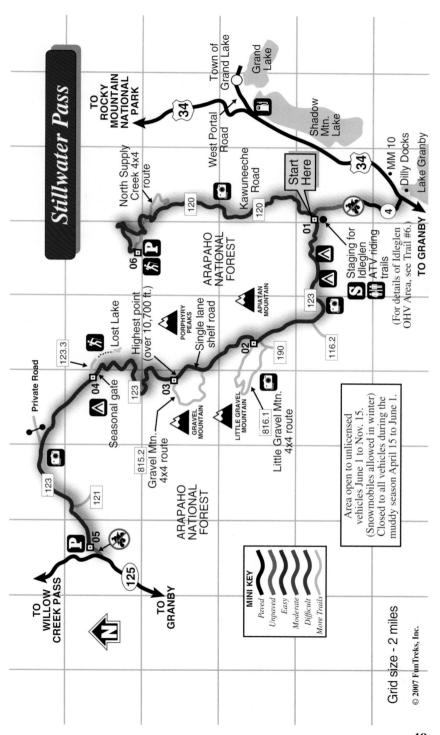

Stillwater Pass

TO ROCKY MOUNTAIN NATIONAL PARK

Town of Grand Lake

Grand Lake

34

West Portal Road

Shadow Mtn. Lake

Kawuneeche Road

North Supply Creek 4x4 route

120

ARAPAHO NATIONAL FOREST

Start Here

120

01

34

MM 10

Dilly Docks

Lake Granby

Staging for Idleglen ATV riding trails

S

123

APIATAN MOUNTAIN

4

TO GRANBY

(For details of Idleglen OHV Area, see Trail #6.)

06

116.2

190

02

Porphyry Peaks

Highest point (over 10,700 ft.)

Lost Lake

123.3

Single lane shelf road

Private Road

123

Seasonal gate

04

03

GRAVEL MOUNTAIN

816.1

LITTLE GRAVEL MOUNTAIN

Little Gravel Mtn. 4x4 route

815.2

Gravel Mtn. 4x4 route

ARAPAHO NATIONAL FOREST

123

121

05

P

125

TO WILLOW CREEK PASS

N

TO GRANBY

Area open to unlicensed vehicles June 1 to Nov. 15. (Snowmobiles allowed in winter) Closed to all vehicles during the muddy season April 15 to June 1.

MINI KEY
Paved
Unpaved
Easy
Moderate
Difficult
More Trails

Grid size - 2 miles

© 2007 FunTreks, Inc.

49

Plenty of dispersed camp spots along Stillwater Pass Road and marked side roads.

Trailheads are well marked.

Steep, tight turns in places.

Crossing narrow bridge with 48″-wide ATV.

Intermittent rocky challenges.

Ride with friends for fun & safety.

Idleglen OHV Area ⬦6

Getting There: From Highway 34 south of Grand Lake (0.3 miles south of mile marker 10 across from Dilly Docks), take County Road 4 northwest. This road starts paved, then changes to gravel. After 3 miles, bear left on Stillwater Pass Road 123. (Staging area is just ahead.)

Staging/Camping: The staging area is huge; however, it still gets crowded on busy summer weekends. If camping, continue past the staging area to numerous dispersed camping spots along Stillwater Pass Road and side roads. Close-in camp spots fill up quickly.

Difficulty: Varies from easy to very difficult. Spruce-Em-Up-Jack Trail is very narrow in spots with tight, steep turns. Bull Mountain is wide but has giant mud holes, most of which can be bypassed. Trail Creek Loop is steep, rocky and narrow. The upper portion of Beaver Line Loop is extremely narrow and winds tightly through the trees.

Highlights: The trails described here are only a sample of the many trails available. Skilled riders will find many challenges if they explore the entire trail system. Although trailheads are well-marked, it is still easy to get confused as you get deeper into the forest. Don't ride alone. Beginners should stay on main roads at first.

Time & Distance: The route described is 18.8 miles and takes about 3 hours depending upon riding skills. Allow a long weekend to ride the entire trail system.

Trail Description: Challenges begin immediately as you wind tightly through the trees above Stillwater Pass Road. The next leg starts easy, but can be difficult during long rainy periods. A steep descent down Trail Creek Loop leads to relatively easy Beaver Line Loop Trail. Return along a narrow twisting trail with many bridges before one final narrow climb back to Stillwater Pass Road. No vehicles wider than 48."

Services: Modern vault toilet at Idleglen staging area. Gas at general store on corner of Highway 34 and West Portal Road. Many services in town of Grand Lake.

Special Map: Arapaho National Forest OFF-HIGHWAY VEHICLE MAP of Stillwater Pass Area. Contact Sulphur Ranger District.

Directions: *(Shadowed portion of trail is described here.)*

WP	Mile	Action
01	0.0	N40° 13.52´ W105° 53.55´ Find Spruce-Em-Up Jack Trailhead on north side of staging area. Head north then immediately swing left.
	2.3	Stay right. Left goes back to main road.
	2.7	Bear right after passing through opening in fence. Left goes back to main road.
	2.8	Stay right through open area with camp spots.
02	3.5/0.0	N40° 13.62´ W105° 55.89´ Spruce-Em-Up Jack ends. Bear right across Stillwater Pass Road to start of wider Bull Mtn. Trail on left.
	1.6	After maneuvering around large mud holes, make sharp right uphill on narrower trail.
03	3.8/0.0	N40° 13.30´ W105° 56.07´ Turn left to connect to Trail Creek Loop Trail. Road gets very rocky. Continue straight, ignoring roads to right that connect to Stillwater Pass Road.
04	0.8	N40° 13.53´ W105° 56.76´ Roads converge. Bear left. Stillwater Pass Road is to right.
	1.1	Pass through fence at start of Trail Creek Loop. Narrow trail weaves steeply downhill.

WP	Mile	Action
05	1.5/0.0	N40° 13.52´ W105° 57.12´ Reach better road at bottom of hill. Stay left then immediately bear right to find narrow bridge that leads to Beaver Line Loop Trail.
05	3.6/0.0	After riding clockwise around Beaver Line Loop, return to Waypoint 05. Head north following signs to Lower Gilsonite Trail. Road quickly narrows to ATV trail with series of bridges, then widens again.
	0.8	Make hard right uphill on marked 116.2.
06	1.2	N40° 13.69´ W105° 56.79´ Make hard left through fence on M115 to Lower Gilsonite Trail. This trail is very narrow, steep and tight through trees. (To bypass M115, continue straight 0.1 miles to Stillwater Pass Road.)
07	1.9	N40° 14.19´ W105° 56.87´ You reach Stillwater Pass Road 123. Right takes you back to staging area in 4.5 miles. (Note: If you are not ready to quit for the day, cross road and head north on Lower Gilsonite Trail.)
01	6.4	Arrive back at staging area.

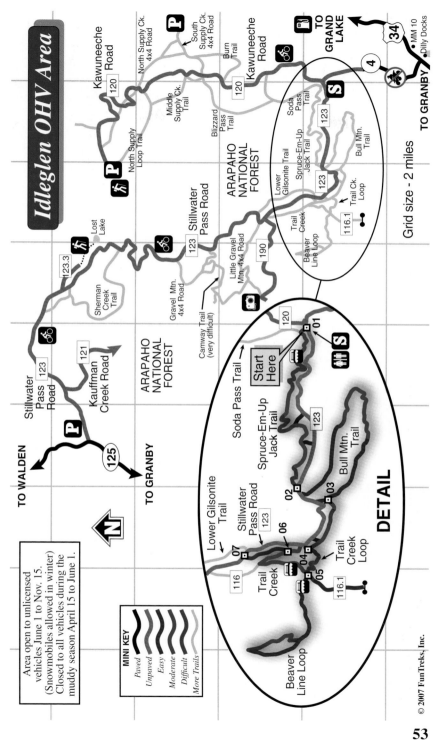

Idleglen OHV Area

Area open to unlicensed vehicles June 1 to Nov. 15. (Snowmobiles allowed in winter) Closed to all vehicles during the muddy season April 15 to June 1.

MINI KEY
Paved
Unpaved
Easy
Moderate
Difficult
More Trails

N

TO WALDEN

TO GRANBY

125

P

Stillwater Pass Road 123

Kauffman Creek Road 121

ARAPAHO NATIONAL FOREST

123.3

Lost Lake

Sherman Creek Trail

P

Kawuneeche Road 120

North Supply Loop Trail

North Supply Ck. 4x4 Road

South Supply Ck. 4x4 Road

P

Middle Supply Ck. Trail

Burn Trail

Kawuneeche Road 120

TO GRAND LAKE

34

MM 10
Dilly Docks

TO GRANBY

4

S

Blizzard Pass Trail

ARAPAHO NATIONAL FOREST

Soda Pass Trail

123

Spruce-Em-Up Jack Trail

Bull Mtn. Trail

123

Lower Gilsonite Trail

Trail Ck. Loop

116.1

Beaver Line Loop

190

Little Gravel Mtn. 4x4 Road

Gravel Mtn. 4x4 Road

Camway Trail (very difficult)

Stillwater Pass Road 123

Trail Creek

Grid size - 2 miles

DETAIL

Start Here

Soda Pass Trail

120

01

S

Spruce-Em-Up Jack Trail

123

Bull Mtn. Trail

02

03

Lower Gilsonite Trail

Stillwater Pass Road 123

06

07

116

Trail Creek

04

05

116.1

Trail Creek Loop

Beaver Line Loop

© 2007 FunTreks, Inc.

53

Many camp spots along route at south end. Some can accommodate large groups.

Please close this cattle gate after passing through.

Novice riders may need help.

Mountain views like this can be seen from a few high points along the route.

Pierson Park Road

Getting There: From Highway 7 at Meeker Park, turn east on Cabin Creek Road, County Road 82. (Meeker Park is south of Estes Park between mile markers 11 and 12.) Go east on Cabin Creek Road 0.9 miles to T intersection and turn right on County Road 82E. Continue another 1.1 miles to Pierson Park Road, F.S. 119, on left. Head uphill through seasonal forest gate and pick from a variety of spots to unload.

Staging/Camping: Camping and unloading area begins inside seasonal forest gate at start of trail. The first mile or so of the route has numerous shaded camping spots, some very large—a great place to go if you have a large group.

Difficulty: A mix of easy and moderate terrain. Two short sections are fairly steep and rocky. Novice riders may need some assistance and/or encouragement to get past these two points.

Highlights: Out-and-back route offers moderate challenges as it winds through Roosevelt National Forest south of Estes Park. The area, adjacent to Rocky Mountain National Park, is scenic but views are limited to a few high points along the route. Pierson Park Road can also be accessed from the north end, but your transport vehicle must climb a steep rocky road to small parking area beyond a residential development.

Time & Distance: Round trip is 16.5 miles. Allow 3 to 4 hours depending on riding skills.

Trail Description: The route begins on a wide road that crosses gentle terrain then climbs north into forest. A steep, rocky descent follows cattle gate as you drop downhill and cross scenic meadow. A rocky, steep climb follows and leads to a loop around Pierson Park. F.S. 119 continues short distance past loop to views of south Estes Park.

Other Nearby Route: The west end of Johnny Park Road, Trail #8, is very close to the start of Pierson Park Road. Unfortunately, you can't ride an ATV on County Road 82E. Load up and go another 1.2 miles on 82E to Johnny Park Road on right.

Services: Meeker Park Lodge on Hwy. 7, just south of Cabin Creek Rd., has a small store but no gas. Full services in Estes Park and Lyons.

Directions: *(Shadowed portion of trail is described here.)*

WP	Mile	Action
01	**0.0**	*N40° 14.08´ W105° 29.94´* From seasonal forest gate, head north on wide road. Road gradually narrows and begins to climb.
02	**1.2**	*N40° 14.88´ W105° 29.85´* Bear hard right past wide road to left. Road gets steeper and rockier.
	3.2	Pass through cattle gate and close it.
03	**4.0**	*N40° 16.48´ W105° 29.61´* Begin steep, rocky descent.
	5.7	Continue north across long, scenic meadow.
04	**6.1**	*N40° 17.62´ W105° 29.63´* Road climbs steeply out of meadow.
	6.6	Continue straight as lesser roads branch off. Open space to right is camping opportunity.
05	**6.7**	*N40° 18.04´ W105° 29.47´* Stay right where 119D goes left. This is southern end of loop.
	6.8	Continue north. (Road goes right to open space.)
06	**7.8/0.0**	*N40° 18.74´ W105° 29.43´* Turn left on 119D to begin loop. (For southern view of Estes Park, go another half mile on 119 to small overlook. This is where you would park if you started trail on the north end.)
	0.5	Driver's choice. (I stayed right to follow 119E.)
07	**1.3**	*N40° 18.13´ W105° 30.06´* Driver's choice. (I turned left downhill on unmarked road. Straight was rougher.)
	1.6	Return to 119D and turn right.
05	**2.0/0.0**	Return to main route 119. Right goes back the way you came. You may want to explore other marked roads in the area before you head back.
01	**6.7**	Arrive back at start.

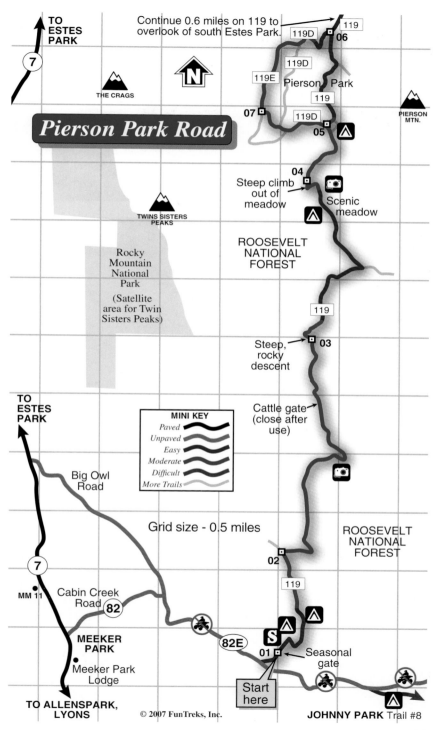

Pierson Park Road

TO ESTES PARK

7

Continue 0.6 miles on 119 to overlook of south Estes Park.

119
119D
06

N

THE CRAGS

119D

119E   Pierson   Park

07   119

119D

05

PIERSON MTN.

04

Steep climb out of meadow

Scenic meadow

TWINS SISTERS PEAKS

Rocky Mountain National Park

(Satellite area for Twin Sisters Peaks)

ROOSEVELT NATIONAL FOREST

119

Steep, rocky descent   03

TO ESTES PARK

7

Cattle gate (close after use)

MINI KEY
Paved
Unpaved
Easy
Moderate
Difficult
More Trails

Big Owl Road

Grid size - 0.5 miles

ROOSEVELT NATIONAL FOREST

02

119

MM 11

Cabin Creek Road   82

MEEKER PARK

82E

S

01   Seasonal gate

Start here

Meeker Park Lodge

TO ALLENSPARK, LYONS

© 2007 FunTreks, Inc.

JOHNNY PARK Trail #8

Plenty of room to camp and unload at eastern end of trail.

Stay on marked trails.

Watch for mountain bikers.

Roughest part of trail is not far from start.

Higher elevation camp spots along trail have views of front range.

Johnny Park Road ◀8▶

Getting There: Take Highway 36 south from Estes Park or north from Lyons. Turn west on County Road 47 about 0.2 miles north of mile marker 11. Follow C.R. 47 west 3 miles and bear left when pavement ends. Start of trail is uphill through gate.

      To ride both Pierson Park Road and Johnny Park Road, follow directions for Trail #7 and ride Johnny Park west to east. ATVs are not allowed on County Road 82E, so you'll have to load up to go from the start of Trail #7 to Trail #8.

Staging/Camping: Large, shaded camping area at start on eastern end. Western end of trail also has a few camp spots. If you are already camping at Trail #7, stay there and transport ATV to Johnny Park.

Difficulty: Mostly easy to moderate; however, eastern end of trail has a couple of difficult steep, rocky sections. The approach to F.S. 118A is also very steep.

Highlights: Convenient day trip from front range. Good weekend adventure when combined with Trail #7. Higher points along route have views of front range. Popular mountain bike route. Be courteous.

Time & Distance: Trail is 5.1 miles one way. Allow 2 to 3 hours to go out and back. F.S. 118A is 0.8 miles one way.

Trail Description: Shortly after heading west from staging area, you encounter a steep, rocky section that novice riders will find very difficult. A few more steep ledges follow before the trail levels out along a high ridge. Choice camp spots through this area have views of front range. This trail once included a section of nasty mud bogs, but these are now closed and the trail has been rerouted around them. F.S. 118A heads northeast from the staging area and climbs steeply to a short network of roads with more camp spots.

Other nearby routes: Pierson Park Road, Trail #7. Also consider Pole Hill, Trail #4, on Highway 36 southeast of Estes Park.

Services: Some services in Lyons and full services in Estes Park. If camping at western end of trail, Meeker Park Lodge, on Highway 7, has a few supplies, but no gas.

Directions: (*Shadowed portion of trail is described here.*)

WP	Mile	Action
01	0.0	***DIRECTIONS EAST TO WEST*** *N40° 14.99´ W105° 24.68´* Head southwest from staging area. Road splits then comes back together. Climb through steep, rocky section.
	0.3	Pass through seasonal forest gate.
	0.9	Another difficult spot.
02	1.0	*N40° 14.86´ W105° 25.38´* Stay left on 118. Good road goes right.
	1.5	Road levels out across high area with many good camp spots, some with views.
03	2.3	*N40° 14.33´ W105° 26.46´* After potential muddy stretch, pass through forest gate.
	2.5	Stay left. Right goes to camp spot.
04	4.4	*N40° 13.68´ W105° 28.28´* Stay right after passing through treed area with shaded camp spots.
	4.9	Another seasonal gate.
05	5.1	*N40° 13.88´ W105° 29.01´* End of Johnny Park Road at County Road 82E.

WP	Mile	Action
05	0.0	***DIRECTIONS WEST TO EAST*** *N40° 13.88´ W105° 29.01´* Bear right off County Road 82E onto Johnny Park Road.
	0.2	Pass through seasonal forest gate.
04	0.7	*N40° 13.68´ W105° 28.28´* Stay left.
	2.6	Continue straight. Lesser road joins on left.
03	2.8	*N40° 14.33´ W105° 26.46´* Pass through seasonal gate. Potential muddy area follows.
	3.6	Cross high area with many good camp spots.
02	4.1	*N40° 14.86´ W105° 25.38´* Stay right on 118.
	4.2	Difficult downhill ledge.
	4.8	Another seasonal gate. Tough spot follows.
01	5.1/0.0	*N40° 14.99´ W105° 24.68´* Drop downhill to large camping and staging area.
06	0.8	***DIRECTIONS FOR 118A*** *N40° 14.62´ W105° 24.12´* Starting at Waypoint 01, continue northeast across parking lot to sign for 118A. Climb steep hill then stay right until trail ends at loop after 0.8 miles.

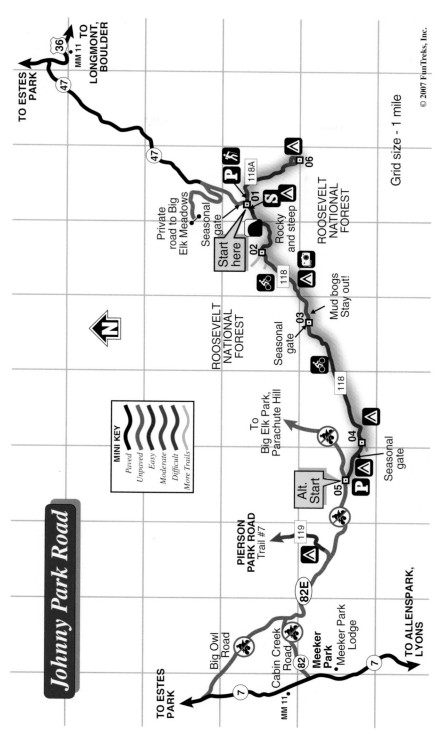

Johnny Park Road

MINI KEY
- Paved
- Unpaved
- Easy
- Moderate
- Difficult
- More Trails

N

TO ESTES PARK

TO LONGMONT, BOULDER

MM 11

36

47

47

TO ESTES PARK

47

Private road to Big Elk Meadows

Seasonal gate

Start here

P

118A

01

S

02

118

Rocky and steep

ROOSEVELT NATIONAL FOREST

06

Mud bogs Stay out!

03

Seasonal gate

118

ROOSEVELT NATIONAL FOREST

04

Seasonal gate

P

To Big Elk Park, Parachute Hill

Alt. Start

05

119

PIERSON PARK ROAD Trail #7

82E

Big Owl Road

Cabin Creek Road

82

MM 11

Meeker Park

Meeker Park Lodge

7

TO ALLENSPARK, LYONS

7

TO ESTES PARK

© 2007 FunTreks, Inc.

Grid size - 1 mile

Historic Bunce School built in 1888.

Many great camp spots. This one is on 216.

Short hike to wreckage. Leave as is.

Ironclads route is steep and rocky in spots.

Steep hike to engine at bottom of hill.

Steep climb to top of Ironclads.

Plane Crash, Ironclads 9

Getting There: Turn west off Highway 7 onto Bunce School Road, located 0.6 miles north of the intersection of Highways 7 and 72 just north of Raymond. Immediately bear left at Bunce School and follow rough road 0.2 miles to wide sandy staging area.

Staging/Camping: Unload at staging area. Many excellent dispersed camp spots along route. If you enter trail from south end on paved C.R. 92, you may camp at developed Peaceful Valley F.S. Campground (reservations recommended). Per campground host, ATVs may travel on paved C.R. 92 short distance to start of F.S. 115 (Wpt. 08).

Difficulty: Bunce School Road, F.S. 115, varies between easy and moderate. The plane crash route is rough but manageable. The Ironclads loop is very difficult in spots. Riding 216A is not recommended.

Highlights: Fun area for all skill levels. Additional marked side roads to explore. See historic Bunce School and wreckage of 1965 plane crash.* Please treat site with respect; two young Air Force officers died here. LEAVE WRECKAGE AS YOU FIND IT. Ironclads route is for advanced riders only. Hike to top of Ironclads for great views.

Time & Distance: Route described here is about 26 miles and takes 3 to 5 hours depending on riding skill. Add time for side roads.

Trail Description: Travel south on Bunce School Road, F.S. 115. Side trip down F.S. 217 connects to network of additional forest roads with many large camp spots. Head north on F.S. 216 to difficult loop below dramatic Ironclads. Farther south on 115, head uphill to plane crash.

Other Nearby Route: Middle St. Vrain OHV Route departs for western end of C.R. 92 after Camp Dick C.G. (Not covered in this book.)

Services: Gas and supplies in Lyons. Full services in Estes Park.

*The plane crash occurred late on Sunday afternoon, June 27, 1965. The T-33A jet trainer was piloted by Air Force Major Jay E. Currie, 39. In the back seat, as technical observer, was 1st Lt. Donald Darby, 25. Both were instructors at Edwards AFB Research Pilot School. They were returning to California from an assignment on the east coast and had just left Buckley Field in Denver after refueling. Major Currie had recently purchased 96 acres of Colorado mountain property and was hoping to see it from the air. He had just spotted the property while flying at 13,000 feet, but at that moment, was ordered to go to 17,000 feet. During discussions with Denver Air Traffic Control out of Longmont as to whether he could stay at that altitude a bit longer, radio contact was lost. This much is known: Currie was a very experienced pilot with over 8700 hours; flaps were down when the plane crashed, indicating he was flying slowly; the crash occurred around 9,300 feet; thunderstorms were reported in the area; neither occupant attempted to eject and the crash investigation found no mechanical problems. Obviously, something unexpected happened at the last second. We will never know for sure what it was. Currie left a wife and three young boys and is buried in Arlington National Cemetery. I was not able to find any personal information on Lt. Darby. *(Information obtained from USAF Accident Report contributed by aviation archaeologist Duke Sumonia.)*

Directions: *(Shadowed portion of trail is described here.)*

WP	Mile	Action
01	**0.0**	*N40° 10.26´ W105° 28.16´* Continue southwest on main road which quickly gets rougher.
02	**0.8**	*N40° 09.99´ W105° 28.64´* F.S. 217 goes left. This road goes downhill 0.8 miles to Hwy. 72. Good camping with side roads to explore.
03	**1.0/0.0**	*N40° 09.92´ W105° 28.77´* Turn right uphill through trees on F.S. 216. Stay right at first.
	0.1	Stay left as roads branch right to camping.
04	**0.6**	*N40° 10.28´ W105° 28.97´* Bear right at fork where loop begins. Road is narrow, steep and rocky in places. Use caution.
	1.2	Stay left and follow loop downhill. F.S. 216A goes right uphill to Ironclads rock outcrop. Recommend you hike this very difficult section.
04	**1.7**	End of loop. Stay right downhill.
03	**2.6/0.0**	Return to Bunce School Road. Turn right.
05	**3.5/0.0**	*N40° 08.17´ W105° 30.30´* After passing through large gate, turn right on one of two closely-spaced roads past camp spot in trees. This becomes F.S. 202.
	0.2	Turn right on F.S. 203, then immediately turn left. Road climbs to plane crash.
06	**2.0**	*N40° 09.32´ W105° 30.52´* Road narrows. Stop here and continue on foot.
07	**2.2**	*N40° 09.49´ W105° 30.38´* Center of crash site. Wreckage spread out up and down steep slopes.
05	**4.4/0.0**	Return to Bunce School Road. Turn right. After another gate, road switchbacks left then right.
08	**0.9**	*N40° 07.91´ W105° 30.56´* Bunce School Road ends at paved C.R. 92. Turn around and retrace route back to start. (Left on C.R. 92 goes to Peaceful Valley Campground. Right goes to Camp Dick Campground and Middle St. Vrain OHV route.)

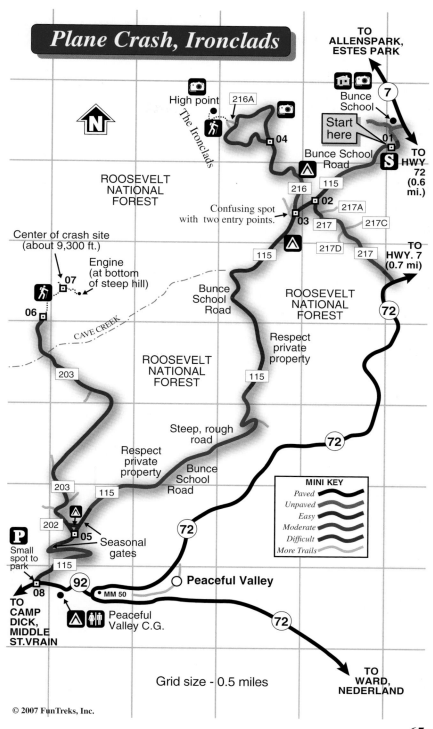

Plane Crash, Ironclads

TO ALLENSPARK, ESTES PARK

High point

216A

04

The Ironclads

Bunce School

Start here

7

01

S

TO HWY 72 (0.6 mi.)

Bunce School Road

216

115

ROOSEVELT NATIONAL FOREST

Confusing spot with two entry points.

02

217A

03

217

217C

Center of crash site (about 9,300 ft.)

Engine (at bottom of steep hill)

07

06

115

217D

217

TO HWY. 7 (0.7 mi)

CAVE CREEK

Bunce School Road

ROOSEVELT NATIONAL FOREST

72

203

ROOSEVELT NATIONAL FOREST

Respect private property

115

72

Steep, rough road

72

Respect private property

Bunce School Road

203

115

202

MINI KEY

Paved
Unpaved
Easy
Moderate
Difficult
More Trails

P

Small spot to park

05

Seasonal gates

115

72

Peaceful Valley

08

92

MM 50

TO CAMP DICK, MIDDLE ST.VRAIN

Peaceful Valley C.G.

72

Grid size - 0.5 miles

TO WARD, NEDERLAND

© 2007 FunTreks, Inc.

65

Walk to ruins at Caribou Townsite.

Crossing Caribou Creek.

Views of Eldora Ski Area.

Rough and muddy in places.

Looking west towards Indian Peaks Wilderness.

Caribou, Eldorado Mtn.

Getting There: From roundabout in Nederland (west of Boulder), take Highway 72 north 0.4 miles. Turn left on Caribou Road, C.R. 128, soon after fire station. Follow 128 uphill 5.3 miles to wide parking area.

Staging/Camping: Unload at wide parking area. No camping here. CAMP IN DESIGNATED SITES ONLY. See map for location of 11 numbered sites. Area is regularly patrolled by local caretaker and rules are enforced. You can also camp at developed Rainbow Lakes F.S. Campground at north end, but you'll have to transport ATV to north entrance since unlicensed vehicles are not allowed on county road.

Difficulty: Mix of easy and moderate routes. Wet conditions can increase difficulty. Steep and rocky in places.

Highlights: Variety of terrain is fun for moderately skilled riders. See scattered ruins of 1869 gold rush town of Caribou.* Popular weekend camping destination close to Boulder. Environmentally sensitive area due to heavy use. Minimum $1,000 fine for riding off existing marked routes. Report violators. Pack out your trash. Douse camp fires.

Time & Distance: Route described here measures 18 miles. Allow 4 to 6 hours. Add time to explore marked side roads.

Trail Description: North on 505 winds through scenic meadow, then gets rougher as it enters forest and crosses Caribou Creek. South on 505 climbs to high point, then descends over varied terrain to residential area near Eldora. Marked side roads lead to mines, designated camp spots and a variety of scenic viewpoints.

Other Nearby Routes: Plane Crash, Ironclads, Trail #9, located north on Highway 72. Rollins Pass East, Trail #12, located south of Nederland off Highway 119.

Services: Full services in Nederland. Nothing along trails.

---

*Miners from all over the world flocked to the town of Caribou after a rich silver deposit was discovered in 1869. Development of the town was rapid. Before long there were houses, stores, hotels, dance halls, blacksmith shops, numerous businesses and a weekly newspaper. It is estimated that $8 million was extracted from these hills in little more than a decade. Most of the mining was done on the northeast side of Caribou Hill. There are still privately owned, active mines in the area. Stay off private property or expect to be caught by a diligent caretaker.

Directions: *(Shadowed portion of trail is described here.)*

WP	Mile	Action
01	**0.0**	*NORTH ROUTE* *N39° 58.86´ W105° 34.74´* Head north on F.S. 505 through open seasonal gate left of kiosk.
02	**0.7**	*N39° 59.43´ W105° 34.54´* Continue straight. (Rougher road to left goes to mine at end of loop and secluded camp spots 6 and 7. Adds 1.3 miles.)
	1.8	Enter forest after passing camp spots 8-11. Road gets rougher.
	2.1	Come out of forest and pass through deeply rutted, potentially muddy section.
	2.2	Cross Caribou Creek. Can be deep in spring.
03	**3.0**	*N40° 00.36´ W105° 33.69´* Road ends at county road. Turn around and return the way you came. Rainbow Lakes Campground is 1/2 mile to left, but ATVs are not allowed on county road.
01	**6.0/0.0**	*SOUTH ROUTE* Return to staging area. Head west downhill into forest on F.S. 505 through open seasonal gate.
	0.3	Boarded-up mine adit to left. Danger, keep out.
	0.5	Stay left uphill on 505 past camp spots 1 and 2. (Right goes to camp spots 3 and 4 then dead ends after 0.5 miles at camp spot 5.)
	0.9	After exiting trees, continue straight on 505 as private road crosses. Climb steep, rocky hill.
04	**1.3**	*N39° 58.65´ W105° 35.53´* Reach top of hill with views. Turn left downhill. (Right climbs to great viewpoint in rock outcrop after very steep hill. Adds 1 mile.)
	1.3+	As you drop downhill, stay right. (Roads to left are eventually gated to stop people from entering back side of Caribou Townsite. $1,000 fine.)
	1.7	Bear left. Then at next intersection, bear right.
	4.4	After crossing rocky Caribou Flats, road narrows and descends steep, tippy switchbacks.
05	**6.0**	*N39° 57.03´ W105° 34.10´* After narrow ledge road, trail ends at seasonal gate above residential area. Turn around and return the way you came.

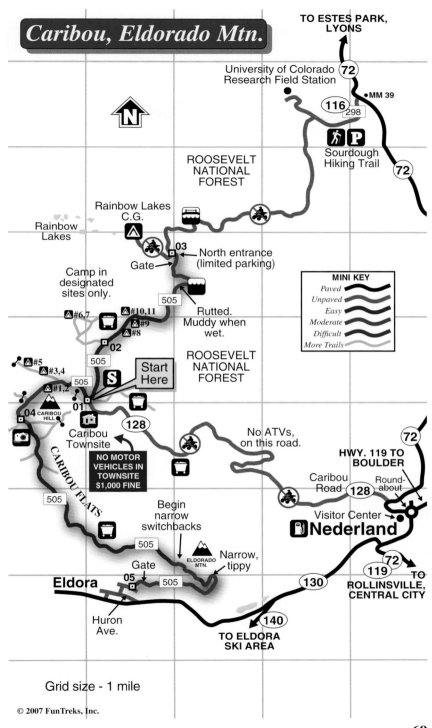

Caribou, Eldorado Mtn.

TO ESTES PARK, LYONS

University of Colorado
Research Field Station

72

116
298

MM 39

72

Sourdough
Hiking Trail

ROOSEVELT
NATIONAL
FOREST

Rainbow Lakes
C.G.

Rainbow
Lakes

03

North entrance
(limited parking)

Gate

Camp in
designated
sites only.

505

Rutted.
Muddy when
wet.

#6,7

#10,11

#9

#8

02

ROOSEVELT
NATIONAL
FOREST

505

#5

#3,4

505

#1,2

S

Start
Here

01

04 CARIBOU
HILL

128

No ATVs,
on this road.

Caribou
Townsite

HWY. 119 TO
BOULDER

72

NO MOTOR
VEHICLES IN
TOWNSITE
$1,000 FINE

Caribou
Road

128

Round-
about

CARIBOU FLATS

Visitor Center

Nederland

505

Begin
narrow
switchbacks

505

ELDORADO
MTN.

Narrow,
tippy

72

Gate

05

505

130

119

TO
ROLLINSVILLE,
CENTRAL CITY

Eldora

Huron
Ave.

140

TO ELDORA
SKI AREA

MINI KEY
Paved
Unpaved
Easy
Moderate
Difficult
More Trails

N

Grid size - 1 mile

© 2007 FunTreks, Inc.

69

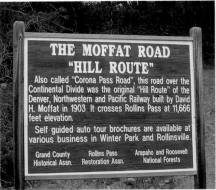

THE MOFFAT ROAD
"HILL ROUTE"

Also called "Corona Pass Road", this road over the Continental Divide was the original "Hill Route" of the Denver, Northwestern and Pacific Railway built by David H. Moffat in 1903 It crosses Rollins Pass at 11,666 feet elevation.

Self guided auto tour brochures are available at various business in Winter Park and Rollinsville.

Grand County   Rollins Pass   Arapaho and Roosevelt
Historical Assn.   Restoration Assn.   National Forests

Look for this sign at start.

Optional Broken Thumb Trail.

Main road passes within a few feet of the Trestle at Rifflesight Notch. Stay off!

Short hike to Twin Trestles from east side.

Outstanding views above timberline.

Rollins Pass West ⑪

Getting There: From Hwy. 40, about 1.5 miles south of Winter Park, turn east on County Road 80. Look for sign shown on opposite page.

Staging/Camping: No place to park first half mile. After that, the road widens in a few places. Don't block road. The best place to unload is at 3.5 miles. Look left for a small road that leads to a clearing where parking and camping are permitted.

Difficulty: Easy. Main road is wide and graded with a few minor rough spots. Optional Boulder Wagon Road, near pass, is moderate with just one mildly rocky section. Optional Broken Thumb Trail is narrow but mostly easy except for two short sections that are difficult (see map).

Highlights: Road follows historic 1903 railroad route and features three outstanding trestles—two in excellent condition (hiking required). Boulder Wagon Road adds much interest to the trip and is not as difficult as it appears. Broken Thumb Trail is only difficult when accessed from the south end. To avoid difficult portion, access trail from bridge at end of F.S. Road 128.1B. Far north end of Broken Thumb Trail has one dangerous tippy spot before narrowing to a hiking trail.

Time & Distance: Main road measures about 14 miles one way. Allow 3 to 4 hours for round trip. Add time for optional routes.

Trail Description: Easy road climbs through forest then continues above timberline to 11,660 feet. Stunning views of Winter Park Ski Area and high mountain lakes. Extend trip by continuing over Boulder Wagon Road to other side of pass. This road takes you to the east side of twin trestles and shortens hike considerably. It also provides views of Rollins Pass East, Trail #12, Yankee Doodle Lake and north side of Needle's Eye Tunnel.

Other nearby routes: Jones Pass, Trail #13, south of Berthoud Pass on Hwy. 40. Bill Moore Lake, Trail # 14, south on Hwy. 40 at Empire. Rollins Pass East, Trail #12. (Note: Because Needle's Eye Tunnel is closed, you cannot ride down Rollins Pass East from the west side. You must access Rollins Pass East from Rollinsville.

Services: Full services in Winter Park, a great summer destination.

Directions: (*Shadowed portion of trail is described here.*)

WP	Mile	Action
01	0.0	N39° 53.87´ W105° 46.16´ Turn northeast off Highway 40, south of Winter Park, and start up County Road 80. No room to unload here.
	0.6	First wide spot with just enough room for one vehicle. Hard to turn around. Wider spots follow next few miles.
02	3.5	N39° 54.92´ W105° 45.61´ Small road joins on left which leads to clearing where you can unload. Camp here, too.
03	3.7/0.0	N39° 54.96´ W105° 45.48´ F.S. 128 crosses. Continue straight on F.S. 149 for main route. (Right goes back to Hwy. 40. Left goes north and quickly connects to F.S. 128.1B. This road leads to a small bridge that connects to easy entry point for Broken Thumb Trail.)

WP	Mile	Action
04	2.7	N39° 53.86 W105° 43.89´ Continue straight. (Other entry point for Broken Thumb Trail is on left—a fun alternative to main road, but has some difficult spots.)
05	3.1	N39° 53.71 W105° 43.40´ Continue straight on main road. (Broken Thumb Trail rejoins main road on left.)
	6.6	Pass Rifflesight Notch Trestle.
	9.4	Hiking trail to Corona Lake on left.
06	10.2	N39° 55.96 W105° 40.99´ Continue straight to Rollins Pass. (Right goes over Boulder Wagon Road 1.6 miles to other side of pass.)
07	10.4	N39° 56.11 W105° 40.92´ Road ends at Rollins Pass (also called Corona Pass) with large area to park and turn around. Hike from here to Twin Trestles. (Note: If you go over Boulder Wagon Road, it is a much shorter hike to other end of trestles and Needle's Eye Tunnel.)

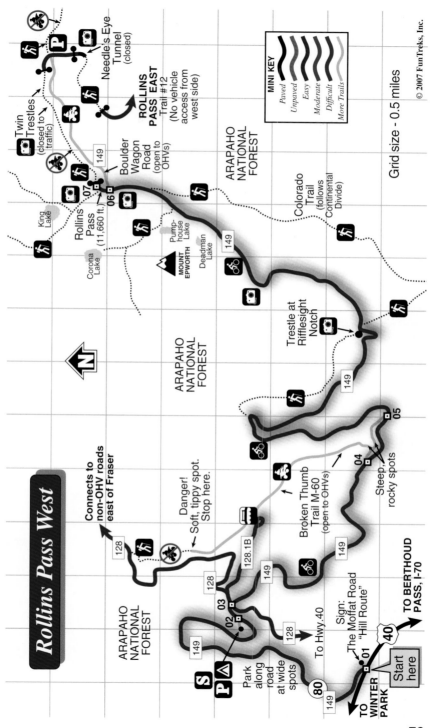

Rollins Pass West

MINI KEY
Paved
Unpaved
Easy
Moderate
Difficult
More Trails

© 2007 FunTreks, Inc.

Grid size - 0.5 miles

N

Needle's Eye Tunnel (closed)

Twin Trestles (closed to traffic)

ROLLINS PASS EAST
Trail #12
(No vehicle access from west side)

149

Boulder Wagon Road (open to OHVs)

07

06

ARAPAHO NATIONAL FOREST

Rollins Pass (11,660 ft.)

King Lake

Corona Lake

MOUNT EPWORTH

Deadman Lake

Pump-house Lake

149

Colorado Trail (follows Continental Divide)

Trestle at Rifflesight Notch

149

ARAPAHO NATIONAL FOREST

05

Broken Thumb Trail M-60 (open to OHVs)

04

Steep, rocky spots

149

Connects to non-OHV roads east of Fraser

128

Danger! Soft, tippy spot. Stop here.

128

128.1B

149

03

02

149

128

ARAPAHO NATIONAL FOREST

S   P

Park along road at wide spots

To Hwy. 40

Sign: The Moffat Road "Hill Route"

01

Start here

80

149

40

TO WINTER PARK

TO BERTHOUD PASS, I-70

73

Wide area to park at start. Don't block traffic on main road.

Looking east as you begin to climb.

Road ends at barricade. Hike from here.

Wildflowers at Yankee Doodle Lake.

Needle's Eye Tunnel is closed.

View of Yankee Doodle Lake as you continue to climb main road towards tunnel.

Rollins Pass East

Getting There: From small town of Rollinsville on Highway 119, head west on County Road 16 (F.S. 149). Continue west after Tolland where F.S. 176 goes left. After total of 7.3 miles, watch for Moffat Road on right. Reverse direction and begin climb here.

Staging/Camping: Unload along road at wide spot near start. Don't block traffic. You can also park at nearby dispersed camping area in trees south of start. Another good place to camp is on right 5.5 miles up Moffat Road. For developed camping, check out Kelly Dahl F.S. Campground located 1 mile north of Rollinsville on Highway 119.

Difficulty: Main route is very easy. Optional Jenny Creek Road 502 winds in and out of rocky Jenny Creek and is difficult in spots.

Highlights: Road follows historic 1903 railroad route and features two lakes, stunning views and an easy hike to Needle's Eye Tunnel.* You can climb over the top of tunnel and continue hike to Twin Trestles.

Time & Distance: Gate at top is 12.3 miles from start. Allow 3 to 4 hours for round trip. Add an extra hour for optional Jenny Creek.

Trail Description: Wide road climbs gently with occasional narrow and rough spots. Upper end of Jenny Creek Road joins main road on right as you start around Yankee Doodle Lake. Jenny Lake can't be seen from main road until you climb above it. Road ends at barricaded gate. Hike along road another 0.6 miles to Needle's Eye Tunnel.

Other nearby routes: Caribou, Eldorado Mountain, Trail #10, is located north on Highway 119 at Nederland. Yankee Hill, Kingston Peak, Trail #15, can be accessed from north end by turning left on F.S. 176 after Tolland.

Services: Full services in Nederland. Store in Rollinsville but no gas.

---

*The original plan for the railroad called for a 2.6-mile tunnel to be built near 10,000 ft. When money ran out, the rails were reluctantly laid over the pass at 11,660 ft. The railroad struggled for many years due to the incredible expense of keeping the route cleared of snow. The modern-day, 6.2-mile Moffat Tunnel was built at a much lower altitude in 1927. Nineteen men died building the tunnel, which took over four years to complete. Trip time for trains, however, was cut from 2 1/2 hours to 12 minutes.

In 1988, the Needle's Eye Tunnel was repaired and reopened thanks to the efforts of the Rollins Pass Restoration Association. Unfortunately, two years later, it was closed again because of an injury lawsuit. The tunnel remains in remarkably good condition, and the fight goes on to reopen it.

Directions: *(Shadowed portion of trail is described here.)*

WP	Mile	Action
01	**0.0**	*N39° 54.31´ W105° 37.87´* Head east from start on well-marked Moffat Road. Great views of valley looking back towards Rollinsville.
	5.5	Continue straight. (Small road on right drops steeply downhill to flat camping area. Great spot for large group.)
02	**5.6**	*N39° 55.36´ W105° 36.90´* Continue straight. (Bottom end of Jenny Creek Road 502 is on right. This road is easier ridden from top to bottom. Check signs to make sure route is open.)
03	**9.5**	*N39° 56.26´ W105° 39.17´* Main road curves left around Yankee Doodle Lake. (Lesser F.S. 808 drops downhill on right. This road connects with top of Jenny Creek Road 502. Another road branches off of 808 and goes steeply uphill to left. This controversial back way to pass is absolutely closed.)
04	**10.3**	*N39° 55.90 W105° 39.70´* Continue straight. (A short rocky spur road goes right uphill to Jenny Lake.)
	11.2	Main road swings right up last major switchback past hiking trail to Forest Lakes. Road narrows to one lane, in places, at old railroad cuts.
05	**12.3**	*N39° 56.04 W105° 40.11´* Road ends at gate with giant boulders blocking passage. Park here and hike 0.6 miles to Needle's Eye Tunnel. (To see outstanding Twin Trestles, climb up right side of tunnel and down the other side. Be careful, it is very steep. Hike another quarter mile to parking lot at junction with Boulder Wagon Road on left. Continue north past parking lot as main road curves around to left. Trestles are short distance around the corner.)

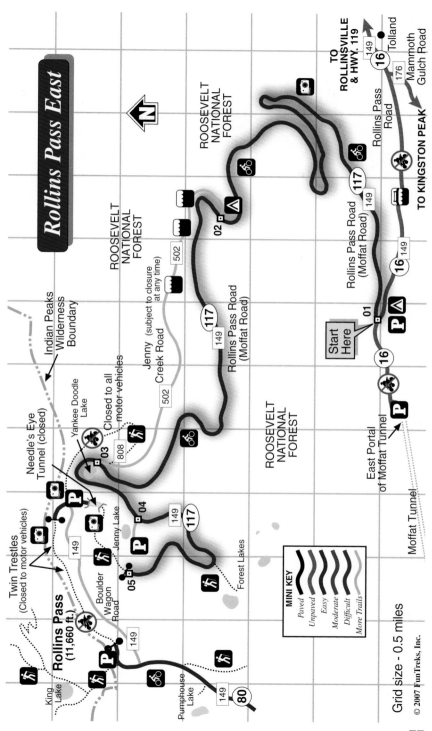

Rollins Pass East

N

Indian Peaks Wilderness Boundary

ROOSEVELT NATIONAL FOREST

ROOSEVELT NATIONAL FOREST

ROOSEVELT NATIONAL FOREST

Needle's Eye Tunnel (closed)

Yankee Doodle Lake

Closed to all motor-vehicles

Jenny (subject to closure at any time)

Creek Road

Rollins Pass Road (Moffat Road)

Twin Trestles (Closed to motor vehicles)

Jenny Lake

Rollins Pass (11,660 ft.)

Boulder Wagon Road

Forest Lakes

King Lake

Pumphouse Lake

Start Here

East Portal of Moffat Tunnel

Moffat Tunnel

Rollins Pass Road (Moffat Road)

Rollins Pass Road

TO ROLLINSVILLE & HWY. 119

Tolland

Mammoth Gulch Road

TO KINGSTON PEAK

MINI KEY
Paved
Unpaved
Easy
Moderate
Difficult
More Trails

Grid size - 0.5 miles

© 2007 FunTreks, Inc.

77

Lower portion of trail as you start up east side.

Snow at pass in early August.

Wildflowers above timberline on east side.

West side descent is steep.

East side view from switchback below pass.

78

Jones Pass

13

Getting There: Take I-70 west from Denver to US 40. Travel northwest on US 40 about 9 miles to tiny town of Berthoud Falls just before a big switchback. Turn left for Henderson Mine *before* going around the bend. (If you miss turn, you can't turn around for quite a distance.) Follow paved road west 1.6 miles. At gate to Henderson Mine, turn right on gravel road, F.S. 144, at sign to Jones Pass. Continue another half mile to wide area where you can park and unload.

Staging/Camping: No camping at start. Dispersed camping along route. See map for best spots.

Difficulty: Great easy route for novice riders. A wide, maintained road but steep in places, especially on the west side. This 12,453-ft. pass is often blocked by snow well into summer. (Top right photo on opposite page was taken August 7.) Snow accumulation varies from year to year. The longer you wait into summer, the better your chances of getting over the pass.

Highlights: Impressive views from very high pass. A short, enjoyable trip even if you can't get over pass. Seasonal wildflowers by stream on east side. Nothing significant to see at bottom of west side, but it is a fun ride. Great hiking at Butler Gulch and along the Continental Divide. Continental Divide hiking trail is also popular with mountain bikers who can ride north all the way to Winter Park.

Time & Distance: Round trip to pass is about 7 miles. Add another 6 miles for round trip down west side. Allow 2 to 3 hours.

Trail Description: Climb gradually through forest to broad views above timberline. Road narrows somewhat as you approach pass, then descends steeply down west side. Closed roads at bottom of west side can be hiked. Side road from Waypoint 02 is rough in places but leads to secluded camp spots. It dead ends in less than a mile.

Other nearby routes: Bill Moore Lake, Trail #14, south on US 40 at Empire. Rollins Pass West, Trail #11, north on US 40 near Winter Park.

Services: Empire has gas and supplies, in addition to a few interesting stores and restaurants. Full services in Winter Park.

Directions: *(Shadowed portion of trail is described here.)*

WP	Mile	Action
01	**0.0**	*N39° 46.25´ W105° 51.23´* Head west uphill from start.
	0.2	Continue straight. (Small parking area on left for Butler Gulch Hiking Trail. Don't use this parking area for staging; it is too small.)
	0.4	Large camp spot on left.
02	**1.0**	*N39° 46.82´ W105° 51.88´* Pass through area of old mines as main road swings left uphill. These mines are private; obey all signs. (Road to right goes to secluded camp spots and dead ends after 0.8 miles. It is rough in places and includes one small stream crossing.)
	1.6	Stay right following main road up switchbacks.
	2.3	Road switchbacks to left. Great photo spot. Look for seasonal wildflowers along small stream to left.
03	**3.5/0.0**	*N39° 46.43´ W105° 53.37´* Jones Pass. Great views in all directions. Hiking trail along continental divide crosses here. (Note: If snow blocks road, park at switchbacks below and hike as far as possible.)
04	**3.0**	*N39° 45.74´ W105° 54.34´* After steep descent down west side on long switchbacks, you reach a T intersection. Road to right is gated closed. Left immediately dead ends between private water department maintenance buildings. Turn around and go back the way you came.

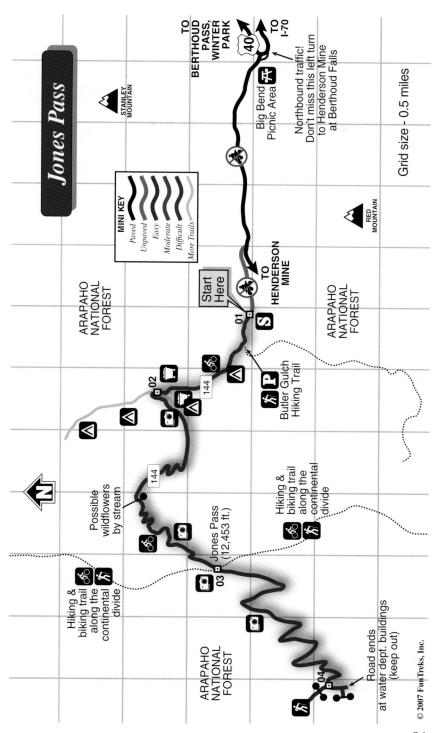

Jones Pass

MINI KEY
- Paved
- Unpaved
- Easy
- Moderate
- Difficult
- More Trails

STANLEY MOUNTAIN

RED MOUNTAIN

TO BERTHOUD PASS, WINTER PARK

TO I-70

40

Big Bend Picnic Area

Northbound traffic! Don't miss this left turn to Henderson Mine at Berthoud Falls

Grid size - 0.5 miles

Start Here

01

TO HENDERSON MINE

S

P
Butler Gulch Hiking Trail

ARAPAHO NATIONAL FOREST

ARAPAHO NATIONAL FOREST

02

144

Possible wildflowers by stream

144

Jones Pass (12,453 ft.)

03

Hiking & biking trail along the continental divide

N

Hiking & biking trail along the continental divide

ARAPAHO NATIONAL FOREST

04

Road ends at water dept. buildings (keep out)

© 2007 FunTreks, Inc.

Remaining structures at Conqueror Mine.

Empire Loop begins steep and rocky.

Crossing Mill Creek at Waypoint 07.

The "Empire Hilton" is open to public.

Bill Moore Lake is located near timberline. Walk short distance from parking area.

Bill Moore Lake, Empire Loop

14

Getting There: Take I-70 west from Denver past Idaho Springs. Head north on Highway 40 about 2 miles to Empire. Turn right at Main Street (North Empire Road) in center of town. Continue uphill beyond pavement. Bear right at fork at 0.7 miles to parking on left at 1.0 miles.

Staging/Camping: Unload at parking lot near fence. No camping here. Plenty of dispersed camping along route (see map). The "Empire Hilton" cabin is free to public on first-come, first-serve basis.

Difficulty: Very rocky and steep in places, especially the route to Bill Moore Lake. The most difficult spot above Waypoint 08 has a bypass.

Highlights: Very scenic route to high mountain lake. Significant remains at Conqueror Mine. Fun route with stream crossings and several old cabins. "Empire Hilton" is functioning cabin with wood-burning stove, beds, blankets, furniture, clothing, food, cooking utensils and interesting pictures on the wall. Please sign guest book inside cabin.

Time & Distance: Total route, including return to start, is 16.8 miles and takes 4 to 5 hours. Allow weekend to explore all roads in area.

Trail Description: Rocky trail goes by Conqueror Mine then climbs to fork at Waypoint 04. Right goes around Empire Loop; left goes directly to Bill Moore Lake. Each route can be ridden separately. Side trip that descends along Miller Creek (different from Mill Creek) ends at narrow, tippy spot where it is difficult to turn around. Difficult optional side trip down Red Elephant Hill ends at base of mountain near Interstate 70. Another side trip, west of Waypoint 07, dead ends in scenic valley. Visit a second cabin (smaller than Empire Hilton) on short side road north of Waypoint 04 (see map). Road to Bill Moore Lake ends at parking lot short of lake. Walk short distance to lake for fishing.

Other nearby routes: Continue north on Highway 40 to Jones Pass, Trail #13, or continue over Berthoud Pass to Rollins Pass West, Trail #11, just before Winter Park. South of Empire, a 4x4 route (not covered in this book) goes to the top of Democrat Mountain.

Services: The small town of Empire has a gas station, post office, local eating spots and a few interesting stores.

Directions: *(Shadowed portion of trail is described here.)*

WP	Mile	Action
01	0.0	*N39° 46.35 W105° 41.03´* Follow road to right along fence after parking area and begin climb.
02	1.3	*N39° 47.02 W105° 40.87´* At Conqueror Mine, make a hard right up steep, narrow spot.
	1.6	Stay right. Very difficult shortcut to left.
	1.9	Main trail turns left and continues to climb. (What looks like camp spot on right is road to scenic overlook.)
03	2.1	*N39° 46.92 W105° 40.57´* Stay right uphill. (Road that joins on left is top of shortcut passed earlier.)
	2.2	Stay left. (F.S. 171.2A goes right to Miller Creek.)
04	2.4	*N39° 47.13´ W105° 40.59´* Stay right on 171.2 to ride Empire Loop first. (Left here on 183.1 is direct route to Bill Moore Lake.)
	2.6	Stay left. (Right goes to interesting cabin in 0.1 miles.)
	3.1	Stay right, then right again to join 171.3.
05	3.5	*N39° 47.44´ W105° 39.86´* Turn left downhill on 171.3 to begin Empire Loop. (Red Elephant Hill is straight ahead.)
	3.9	Stay right downhill. After meadow, cross Mill Creek.
06	5.7	*N39° 48.05´ W105° 39.61´* Empire Hilton on left.
07	7.7	*N39° 48.06´ W105° 40.91´* After rocky descent, turn left at T and cross creek again. (Right dead ends.)
	7.8	Stay left uphill after crossing creek.
	8.5	Turn right away from loop. (Road becomes 171.3C.)
08	8.7/0.0	*N39° 47.54´ W105° 40.62´* Stay right up steep spot on 183.1. (Left returns to Waypoint 04.)
	0.1	Turn right on 183.1A to bypass very difficult spot.
	0.4	Turn right as you rejoin 183.1. Steep spots follow.
	0.8	Stay left. (183.1C goes right.)
09	1.5	*N39° 47.58´ W105° 41.92´* After short descent, stay right on 183.1. (183.1D goes left.)
	1.7	Continue straight. (183.1D rejoins on left.)
	2.0	Long, steep descent followed by mud bog.
10	2.5	*N39° 48.20 W105° 42.63´* Stop at parking lot for Bill Moore Lake. (To return to start, retrace route to Waypoint 08, then turn right to reach Waypoint 04. Continue downhill the way you came.)

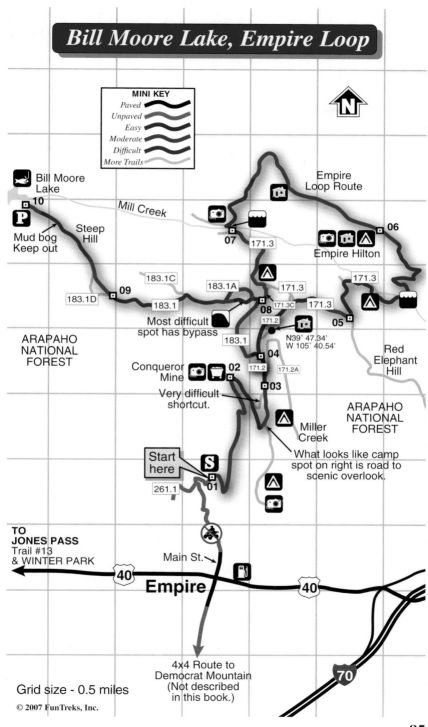

Bill Moore Lake, Empire Loop

MINI KEY
Paved
Unpaved
Easy
Moderate
Difficult
More Trails

N

Bill Moore Lake
10
P
Mud bog
Keep out

Mill Creek

Steep Hill

Empire Loop Route

07
171.3

06

Empire Hilton

183.1C
183.1A
171.3
171.3

09
183.1D
183.1
08
171.3C
171.3
05

Most difficult
spot has bypass
171.2

N39° 47.34'
W 105° 40.54'

ARAPAHO
NATIONAL
FOREST

183.1

Red
Elephant
Hill

Conqueror
Mine
02
171.2
04
171.2A
03

Very difficult
shortcut.

ARAPAHO
NATIONAL
FOREST

Miller
Creek

What looks like camp
spot on right is road to
scenic overlook.

Start
here
261.1

S
01

TO
JONES PASS
Trail #13
& WINTER PARK

Main St.

40
Empire
40

4x4 Route to
Democrat Mountain
(Not described
in this book.)

70

Grid size - 0.5 miles

© 2007 FunTreks, Inc.

85

Large staging area next to Rocky Mountain Cemetery.

Red reflectors mark F.S. 772.1.

View of Loch Lomond from Rockhouse at Wpt. 08.

Route near Kingston Peak.

Wet and rocky on F.S. 772.1 through Miners Gulch.

Family outing is fun for all.

Yankee Hill, Kingston Peak

15

Getting There: From Central City, at the corner of Main Street and Eureka Street, head west uphill on Eureka Street about 1.2 miles and bear left on Bald Mountain Road. In 100 feet, turn right into large staging area next to Rocky Mountain Cemetery. You can unload here or follow signs to Columbine Campground on road just north of staging area.

Staging/Camping: See photo of staging area on opposite page. Columbine F.S. Campground has pit toilets and picnic tables. Some sites can be reserved (see appendix for reservation number). Sign at entrance to campground says no ATVs, but if you are staying there, you are allowed to ride in and out. Plenty of dispersed camping along route.

Difficulty: Main route is moderately steep and rocky in places. Some difficult terrain can be found on side roads. Trip to top of Yankee Hill is very steep and rocky. Many unmarked roads crisscross area, making route-finding confusing at times.

Highlights: A tangle of rugged, remote trails between Central City and Alice. Most of area is between 9,000 and 12,000 feet with sweeping views above timberline. One overlook, near Yankee Hill, looks across valley to St. Mary's Glacier. Another, near Kingston Peak, looks down on scenic Loch Lomond.

Time & Distance: Out-and-back route described here measures 32.5 miles. Allow 5 to 6 hours. Camp overnight for a great weekend.

Trail Description: Trail begins near Central City on mostly easy roads. After a few miles, roads narrow and become rockier. A key fork at Waypoint 04 sends you in two completely different directions. Left goes past Yankee Hill on a more direct route to Alice. Right drops through Miners Gulch to connect with F.S. 353 that takes you over Kingston Peak towards Alice. You must eventually turn around on both routes because ATVs are not allowed to ride through Alice.

Other nearby routes: Rollins Pass East, Trail #12, and Caribou/Eldorado Mountain, Trail #10.

Services: Gas and some services in Central City and Blackhawk. No services in Alice and nearby Apex.

Directions: *(Shadowed portion of trail is described here.)*

WP	Mile	Action
01	0.0	N39° 48.50 W105° 31.92´ From staging area, head west following signs to Columbine C. G.
	1.0	Turn left on lesser F.S. Road 739.1. (Straight goes to campground in 0.2 miles.)
	2.2	Stay left on 739.1 and cross private land.
02	2.6/0.0	N39° 48.17 W105° 34.34´ Turn right and stay on Pisgah Lake Road 175.1.
	1.8	Stay right on 175.2 at open dirt area.
	2.2	At buck & rail fence, go straight on 175.3B. (Hike to interesting grave in field to left.)
03	2.4	N39° 49.70 W105° 35.30´ Major intersection. Turn left uphill on 175.3.
	2.9	Make hard left. Straight is difficult shortcut.
	3.3	Left at top of hill at 4-way intersection.
04	3.5/0.0	N39° 49.78 W105° 36.16´ Key intersection. Stay left on 175.3 to reach Yankee Hill. (Straight goes to Kingston Peak.)
	0.6	Stay left on 175.3. Right is 175.3D.
	1.0	Stay left on 175.3. Unmarked road to right.
	1.1	Stay right. F.S. 271.1 goes left.
05	1.6/0.0	N39° 49.52 W105° 37.52´ Turn left downhill on 171.1D. (Option: Right goes to top of Yankee Hill. Straight goes to overlook of St. Mary's Glacier, then down to town of Alice.
	0.9	Turn left on 271.1 (Cumberland Gulch)
06	1.8	N39° 49.29 W105° 37.10´ Turn right on 271.1F. (Straight returns to 175.3.)
	2.0	Stay right and circle around viewpoint.
	2.4	Continue straight and weave your way back to Waypoint 04.
04	3.7/0.0	Turn left on 772.1. Follow red reflectors on brown posts through Miners Gulch.
	2.3	Right at cabin ruins.
07	3.0/0.0	N39° 51.49 W105° 37.68´ Turn left on F.S. 353 towards Kingston Peak.
	2.1	Bear left up steep hill past hiking trailhead.
08	4.5	N39° 49.69 W105° 39.88´ Rockhouse Overlook—a good place to turn around. (Straight ends above town of Alice.)

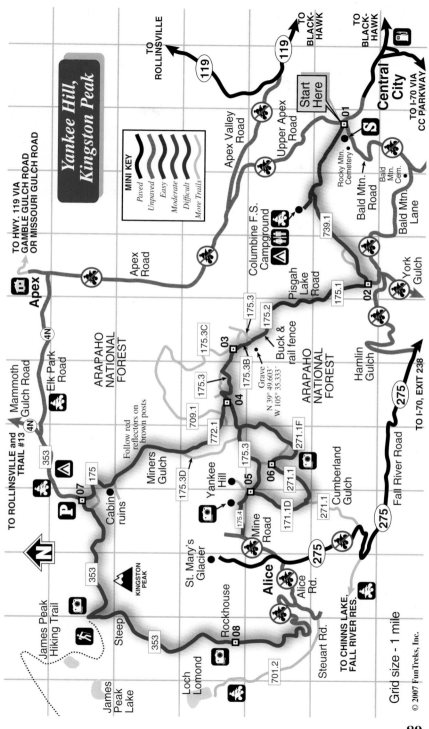

Yankee Hill, Kingston Peak

MINI KEY
Paved
Unpaved
Easy
Moderate
Difficult
More Trails

TO BLACK-HAWK
TO BLACK-HAWK
TO ROLLINSVILLE
119
119
119
Start Here
Central City
TO I-70 VIA CC PARKWAY
01
Rocky Mtn. Cemetery
Bald Mtn. Cem.
Bald Mtn. Road
Bald Mtn. Lane
Apex Valley Road
Upper Apex Road
Columbine F.S. Campground
739.1
Pisgah Lake Road
175.1
02
York Gulch
Apex Road
Apex
TO HWY. 119 VIA GAMBLE GULCH ROAD OR MISSOURI GULCH ROAD
4N
Elk Park Road
Mammoth Gulch Road
4N
ARAPAHO NATIONAL FOREST
175.3
175.2
Buck & rail fence
175.3C
03
175.3B
Grave
N 39° 49.603'
W 105° 35.333'
ARAPAHO NATIONAL FOREST
Hamlin Gulch
TO I-70, EXIT 238
275
Fall River Road
TO ROLLINSVILLE and TRAIL #13
353
175
07
Follow red reflectors on brown posts
Miners Gulch
709.1
175.3
772.1
175.3D
Yankee Hill
04
05
175.3
271.1F
06
271.1
Cumberland Gulch
271.1
275
P
Cabin ruins
171.1D
175.4
Mine Road
275
Alice
Alice Rd.
TO CHINNS LAKE, FALL RIVER RES.
N
353
KINGSTON PEAK
St. Mary's Glacier
Rockhouse
Alice Rd.
Steuart Rd.
James Peak Hiking Trail
353
Steep
08
Loch Lomond
701.2
James Peak Lake
Grid size - 1 mile
© 2007 FunTreks, Inc.

89

Cabin foundations at Lamartine Townsite.

Cabin just south of Wpt. 05 on F.S. 712.2B.

Saxon Road switchbacks above Georgetown.

Route is anything but smooth.

Picnic area at top of Saxon Mountain. Several information boards explain views.

Saxon Mountain, Lamartine

16

Getting There: Get off I-70 at Idaho Springs, Exit 240. Head south on Route 103 towards Mt. Evans. Turn right on Cascade Creek Road 116 about a half mile past mile marker 5. (Note: Previous printing of this book used Ute Creek Road 118 as the entry point for this trail. We found Cascade Creek Road to be a better entrance because parking problems are eliminated and the trail is more fun to drive.)

Staging/Camping: There is a small area to park along Highway 103 before you turn, but better parking is available 0.4 miles up Cascade Creek Road. This stretch of road is a bit rougher and you may need higher ground clearance. There is also a small area to camp at the 0.4-mile point. A small commercial RV park is located on Highway 103 on the way to start of trail.

Difficulty: Route varies from easy to moderate with several rocky sections. Worst stretch is on F.S. 710.1, south of Waypoint 07.

Highlights: Network of old mining roads through historically significant mining area. Look carefully for evidence of the past, not always obvious to a casual observer. Panoramic views from atop 11,546-ft. Saxon Mountain. Descend dizzying switchbacks to Georgetown. Many legal side roads to explore.

Time & Distance: Basic loop route described here is 12.2 miles and takes 3 to 4 hours. Add 1.2 miles to reach the top of Saxon Mountain. It's about 6 miles down Saxon Road to Georgetown.

Trail Description: You'll climb to hidden Lamartine Townsite located on high ridge. East at Waypoint 04 goes past Lamartine Mine and descends to Lamartine Tunnel. West continues on loop past good camp spots. North side of loop goes past upper end of difficult Spring Creek Jeep Trail. From near Wpt. 07, take side trips downhill to Georgetown or uphill to top of Saxon Mountain. Return to Wpt. 07 and descend rocky road to Cascade Creek Road, which returns to start.

Other nearby routes: Yankee Hill/Kingston Peak, Trail #15, and Bill Moore Lake/Empire Loop, Trail #14.

Services: Full services and many tourist attractions in Idaho Springs and Georgetown. National Forest Visitor Center at I-70 and 103.

Directions: *(Shadowed portion of trail is described here.)*

WP	Mile	Action
01	0.0	N39° 42.38 W105° 36.33´ Head northwest uphill on Cascade Creek Road 116.
	0.4	Small area to park and camp. Continue uphill.
02	1.2	N39° 42.69 W105° 37.53´ Turn hard right uphill on 710.1C
	1.9	Hard right up switchback at flat mine area.
	2.2	Continue straight where road joins on left.
03	2.4	N39° 43.23 W105° 37.12´ Bear left uphill on Ute Creek Road 118.
	2.7	Turn right uphill at large boulder with arrow.
04	4.4/0.0	N39° 43.90 W105° 37.05´ At top of hill, turn left on 712.2. (Note: 727.1B on left goes downhill short distance to Lamartine townsite.)
05	1.1	N39° 43.58 W105° 38.09´ Stay right and continue on 712.2. (Left goes downhill on 712.2B direct to Waypoint 08.)
	1.6	Stay left where 712.2G goes right.
	1.8	Stay right where 712.2I goes left to mine.
	2.4	Continue straight where 712.2G rejoins.

WP	Mile	Action
06	2.6/0.0	N39° 43.92 W105° 38.72´ Continue straight. (Downhill to right is difficult Jeep trail 712.2J.)
	0.6	Bear left. (Right goes to top of Saxon Mountain and Georgetown. See separate directions below.)
07	0.6 + 200 ft.	N39° 43.64 W105° 39.27´ At intersecting roads, stay left (southwest) downhill on 710.1.
	1.6	Make hard left on 710.1 where 710.1A goes straight.
08	2.4	N39° 42.88 W105° 39.11´ At clearing, turn right downhill into trees staying on 710.1.
02	4.0	Return to Waypoint 02 and stay right.
01	5.2	Return to start of trail at Highway 103.
07	0.0	*DIRECTIONS TO SAXON MOUNTAIN* Head north very short distance to 712.2 and turn left.
	0.1	You reach T intersection where 712.2 goes right downhill to Georgetown. To reach top of Saxon Mountain, turn left uphill on 712.2C.
09	1.2	N39° 43.36 W105° 40.32´ Picnic area at top of Saxon Mountain. Turn around here.

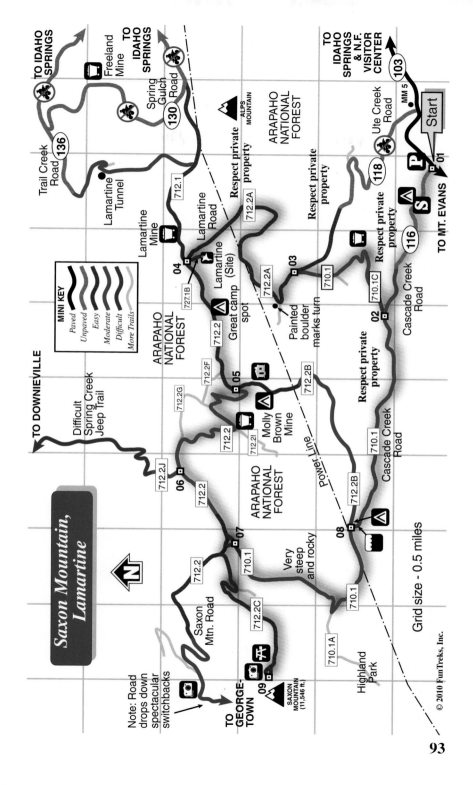

Saxon Mountain, Lamartine

MINI KEY
Paved
Unpaved
Easy
Moderate
Difficult
More Trails

N

TO DOWNIEVILLE

Note: Road drops down spectacular switchbacks

TO GEORGETOWN

SAXON MOUNTAIN (11,546 ft.)

09

712.2C

712.2

Saxon Mtn. Road

07

710.1

06

712.2J

712.2

ARAPAHO NATIONAL FOREST

712.2G

712.2F

712.2I

712.2

Molly Brown Mine

05

712.2

ARAPAHO NATIONAL FOREST

727.1B

04

Lamartine Mine

Lamartine Road

712.1

Lamartine (Site)

Great camp spot

Painted boulder marks turn

712.2A

712.2A

712.2B

712.2B

08

710.1

710.1

710.1

710.1A

Highland Park

Power Line

Cascade Creek Road

Cascade Creek Road

Respect private property

02

710.1C

03

710.1

Respect private property

Respect private property

Respect private property

Respect private property

ALPS MOUNTAIN

ARAPAHO NATIONAL FOREST

118

116

01

Start

P

S

TO MT. EVANS

Ute Creek Road

MM 5

103

TO IDAHO SPRINGS & N.F. VISITOR CENTER

130

Spring Gulch Road

136

Trail Creek Road

Lamartine Tunnel

Freeland Mine

TO IDAHO SPRINGS

TO IDAHO SPRINGS

Difficult Spring Creek Jeep Trail

Grid size - 0.5 miles

© 2010 FunTreks, Inc.

93

Looking south from west end of trail towards Avon and Beaver Creek Ski Area.

Abundant wildflowers in late July, 2006.

Many legal side roads to explore.

Road drops steeply into Berry Creek Canyon.

Road down June Creek Canyon.

Red & White Mountain 17

Getting There: Get off Interstate 70 at Vail, Exit 176. Head west from the north side roundabout on frontage road and turn right on Red Sandstone Road. It heads uphill through residential area and turns hard right up a switchback. After next switchback, stay left on F.S 700 and continue 5.5 miles. After road bends sharply left, look left for camp spots under trees. Use this area for staging. Pull well off road.

Staging/Camping: Parking along the lower, narrower portion of F.S. 700 is prohibited. Please wait until you reach staging area described above. More dispersed camping is available past staging area. Piney Crossing Campground is very small and fills up quickly.

Difficulty: Most of this route is easy except for a moderate stretch between Waypoints 03 and 06. Explore other roads with great caution as difficult spots occur without warning. Berry Creek Canyon is for experts only and should never be ridden alone.

Highlights: Stunning views of Vail and Beaver Creek Ski Areas looking south. Great hiking and seasonal wildflowers. Exciting, moderate descent down June Creek Canyon. Impressive overlook below Wpt. 04.

Time & Distance: Route described here is about 48 miles and takes 4 to 5 hours. Spend an entire weekend exploring other marked roads.

Trail Description: Follow a gorgeous red dirt road high into the mountains above beautiful Vail, CO. Unload and begin scenic loop west. The farther west you go, the rougher and more remote the trail becomes. Several roads descend south from F.S. 734, but all dead end. Moderate June Creek Canyon is one of the best. Explore a network of varied roads west from the bottom of June Creek Canyon. Trail 1881 is exclusively for ATVs and dirt bikes. Many more miles of roads to explore west of Waypoint 07. Northern portion of loop on F.S. 700 is easy.

Other nearby routes: Head south on Highway 24 west of Vail to Camp Hale Area, Trail #21. (FYI: West of Camp Hale is notorious Holy Cross Jeep Trail, described in *Guide to Colorado Backroads & 4-Wheel Drive Trails, 2nd Edition.*)

Services: Gas and supplies in Vail.

Directions: (*Shadowed portion of trail is described here.*)

WP	Mile	Action
01	0.0	N39° 41.38 W106° 25.39´ Head west on wide F.S. 700 from staging area.
02	1.0/0.0	N39° 41.83 W106° 26.13´ Turn left on F.S. 734 following sign to Red & White Mountain.
	2.1	Make a sharp right turn where road continues straight to Buffehr Hiking Trail.
	4.4	Follow main road as it curves right.
03	6.0	N39° 40.81 W106° 28.21´ At meadow, stay left on lesser road. Right goes uphill to viewpoint.
	9.2	Stay right (779 goes left downhill into trees). Main road soon opens up with great views.
04	9.9	N39° 41.98 W106° 31.39´ Bear left under big tree to take side trip to great overlook.
	10.7	Road ends at overlook to June Creek Canyon. Turn around and go back to Waypoint 04.
04	11.5	Back at Waypoint 04, turn left and continue on 734. Go only 50 feet and turn left again.
05	12.3	N39° 42.33 W106° 31.91´ Short, rocky hill drops down to "T" intersection. Turn left on 717 to descend June Creek Canyon.

WP	Mile	Action
	17.5	Turn around just past seasonal gate. (Option: Explore network of fun roads to west that connect to bottom of Berry Creek Canyon.)
05	22.7/0.0	Back to top at Waypoint 05, continue to left.
06	0.7/0.0	N39° 42.48 W106° 32.50´ Stay right to continue on 734. (Left goes downhill towards Berry Creek Canyon. Road starts easy, then gets dangerously steep after 1.8 miles.)
	200 ft.	Continue straight to stay on 734. (Option: Right is more difficult shortcut to F.S. 700. Roads are poorly marked and confusing.)
	0.6	Stay right. (Optional ATV Trail 1881 goes left.)
	1.2	Continue straight. (F.S. 433 joins on right.)
07	2.8/0.0	N39° 43.65 W106° 34.43´ Turn right on F.S. 700. (Left goes to Muddy Pass and beyond.)
08	4.8	N39° 43.65 W106° 30.96´ Continue straight. (F.S. 433 joins on right. This is exit point of shortcut mentioned earlier.)
	14.6	Turn right at major intersection. (Left goes to Piney Crossing Campground and Piney Lake.)
02	14.7	Continue straight back to staging area.

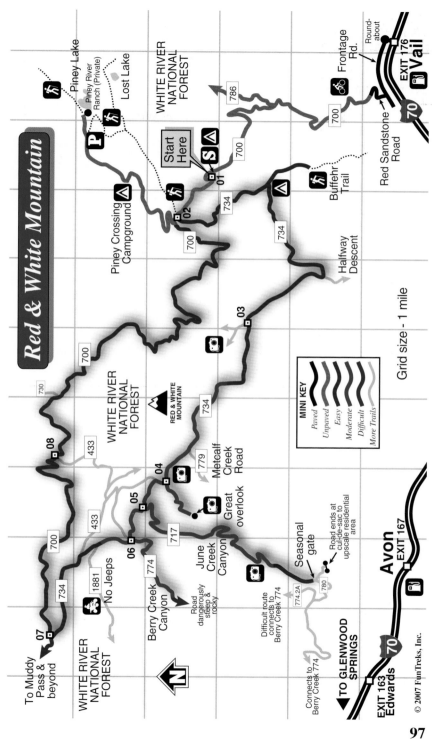

Red & White Mountain

Start Here

WHITE RIVER NATIONAL FOREST

Piney Lake

Piney River Ranch (Private)

Lost Lake

Piney Crossing Campground

Buffehr Trail

Vail

EXIT 176

Frontage Rd.

Round-about

Red Sandstone Road

Halfway Descent

786

700

01

02

700

734

734

734

700

03

730

08

433

WHITE RIVER NATIONAL FOREST

RED & WHITE MOUNTAIN

779

Metcalf Creek Road

04

Great overlook

05

433

717

06

700

734

1881

No Jeeps

774

Berry Creek Canyon

Road dangerously steep & rocky

June Creek Canyon

Seasonal gate

Road ends at cul-de-sac to upscale residential area

780

774.2A

Difficult route connects to Berry Creek 774

Connects to Berry Creek 774

07

To Muddy Pass & beyond

WHITE RIVER NATIONAL FOREST

MINI KEY
Paved
Unpaved
Easy
Moderate
Difficult
More Trails

Grid size - 1 mile

Avon
EXIT 167

Edwards
EXIT 163

TO GLENWOOD SPRINGS

70

N

© 2007 FunTreks, Inc.

97

Main road follows Peru Creek.

Easy ride to Pennsylvania Mine Complex.

Road to upper mine.

Water crossing on optional Chihuahua Gulch.

Poisonous mushrooms.

All mines are private property.

View from top of optional Warden Gulch.

Getting There: Get off Route 6 at east end of Keystone Ski Area, following signs to Montezuma Road. There is an exit ramp for east-bound traffic but westbound traffic must turn left at Gondola Road and backtrack to Montezuma Road (see map detail next page). Head south on Montezuma Road 4.5 miles along the Snake River. When the road curves left, immediately turn left into a fenced parking area.

Staging/Camping: Unload at parking area or at small camping area short distance up trail on right. Read signs for latest trail status. At time of this writing, reclamation work had closed route beyond Pennsylvania Mine. If too wet, route may be closed to motorized traffic.

Difficulty: Main road to Pennsylvania Mine is very easy. Optional side trips up Chihuahua and Warden Gulches are moderate with a few steep, rocky sections. F.S. 260, beyond Shoe Basin Mine, is also steep and rocky. (May be moot point if 260 is closed.)

Highlights: Main road is short but leads to interesting and photogenic structures at the Pennsylvania Mine. Moderately skilled riders should have no problem with optional Chihuahua and Warden Gulches. To extend your day in this beautiful area, add a picnic or hike.

Time & Distance: Trip to Pennsylvania Mine and back is only 8.8 miles and can be done quickly. Allow a half day for all side routes.

Trail Description: Follow main road along Peru Creek past entrance points to Warden and Chihuahua Gulches. Continue uphill past small picnic area to cluster of old mine buildings on right. After crossing creek, road forks to different structures then climbs to upper mine. I highly recommend optional side trip up Chihuahua Gulch. If open, Horseshoe Basin, past Shoe Basin Mine is another great trip.

Other nearby routes: Continue on Montezuma Road less than a mile to small town of Montezuma. After passing through town, continue uphill to a large parking lot. From here you can ride uphill on Deer Creek Trail, an alternate way to Wise Mountain and Radical Hill, Trail #19.

Services: Continue west on Highway 6 into Keystone for gas and convenience stores. There's usually a portable toilet in Montezuma.

Directions: *(Shadowed portion of trail is described here.)*

WP	Mile	Action
01	0.0	*N39° 35.54´ W105° 52.26´* Head north on F.S. 260. Check postings at start for latest trail status. You'll soon pass a small camping area on right with portable toilet.
02	2.0	*N39° 36.03´ W105° 50.41´* Continue straight. (Optional Warden Gulch F.S. 265 goes right, crosses creek, then turns left through camp spots. A steep, rocky climb follows and ends after 2.2 miles at mine below Morgan Peak.)
03	2.1	*N39° 36.03´ W105° 50.29´* Continue straight. (Optional Chihuahua Gulch 263 goes left. Road begins rocky and steep, then gets easier as it twists back and forth across scenic creek. Trail ends after 2.3 miles at popular hiking trail to Grays and Torreys 14,000-ft. peaks.)
04	3.7	*N39° 36.16´ W105° 48.79´* Turn right downhill and cross creek. Small roads branch right then left to mine buildings, part of the private Pennsylvania Mine. Take pictures from road. It is dangerous and illegal to enter or approach buildings.
	4.0	Continue straight up steep, rocky road to upper mine.
05	4.4	*N39° 35.86´ W105° 48.82´* Upper mine to left. Best to turn around here. (Rocky road continues up Cinnamon Gulch but there is not much to see.)
04	5.1	Return to main road at Waypoint 04. (Note: At time of this writing, F.S. 260 was closed to motorized recreation due to reclamation at Shoe Basin Mine. If road is open, you can continue east on 260. Status of trail beyond Shoe Basin Mine to Horseshoe Basin was unknown.)

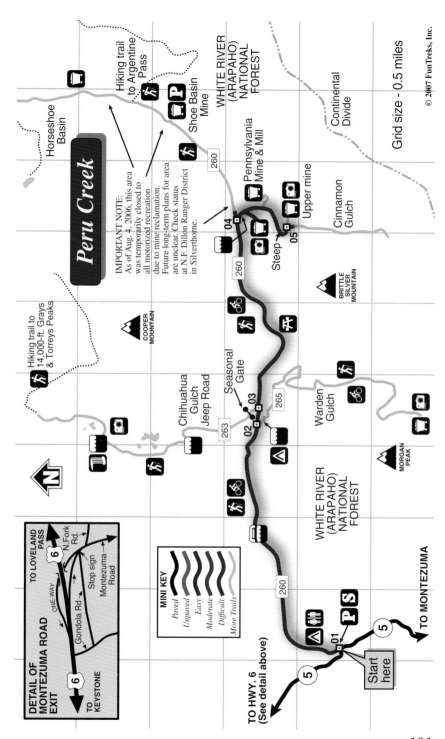

Peru Creek

IMPORTANT NOTE:
As of Aug. 4, 2006, this area was temporarily closed to all motorized recreation due to mine reclamation. Future long-term plans for area are unclear. Check status at N.F. Dillon Ranger District in Silverthorne.

Hiking trail to Argentine Pass

Shoe Basin Mine

WHITE RIVER (ARAPAHO) NATIONAL FOREST

Continental Divide

Horseshoe Basin

Pennsylvania Mine & Mill

Upper mine

Cinnamon Gulch

Steep

BRITTLE SILVER MOUNTAIN

Hiking trail to 14,000-ft. Grays & Torreys Peaks

COOPER MOUNTAIN

Chihuahua Gulch Jeep Road

Seasonal Gate

Warden Gulch

MORGAN PEAK

WHITE RIVER (ARAPAHO) NATIONAL FOREST

N

DETAIL OF MONTEZUMA ROAD EXIT

TO LOVELAND PASS

N. Fork Rd.

ONE-WAY

Gondola Rd.

Stop sign

Montezuma Road

TO KEYSTONE

TO HWY. 6 (See detail above)

MINI KEY
Paved
Unpaved
Easy
Moderate
Difficult
More Trails

Start here

TO MONTEZUMA

Grid size - 0.5 miles

© 2007 FunTreks, Inc.

101

Room for RVs at staging area.

High up Middle Fork of the Swan River.

Rainbow below Wise Mountain.

Chances are good you'll see mountain goats.

Starting up Radical Hill.

Breathtaking scenery in every direction.

Taking a break for lunch at the top of Wise Mountain. Cabin is open to public.

Wise Mountain, Radical Hill

Getting There: From Highway 9, about 4 miles north of Breckenridge, head east on well-marked Tiger Road toward golf course. Go east 4.8 miles to treed area on right. An *alternate entry point*, if you don't need to camp, is south of Montezuma (see map). Follow directions to Peru Creek, Trail #18, but continue 2.3 miles through town to large parking lot at base of Deer Creek Trail. Follow C.R. 5 which becomes F.S. 5.

Staging/Camping: Trail directions start from Tiger Road where you can camp. If first camping area is filled, follow trail directions another 1.5 miles to second camping area on right.

Difficulty: Most of trail is moderate except Radical Hill and upper parts of North and Middle Fork routes, which are steep and rocky in places. Best time to ride is mid to late summer. Snow can block upper parts of trail well into July or even longer in heavy snow years. (See page 15 for carburetor adjustment information.)

Highlights: This is the ultimate ATV adventure. You'll see non-stop, eye-popping scenery, mines, wildflowers and many well-preserved cabins. Much of trail follows the Continental Divide where mountain goat sightings are common. Trails are fun and not overwhelmingly difficult. Riding unlicensed vehicles through Montezuma is strictly forbidden.

Time & Distance: Route described here is 28.4 miles and takes 4 to 5 hours. Allow an entire weekend to explore all routes in area.

Trail Description: Trail starts easy but quickly steepens as you near the Continental Divide. Once on top, trail levels out where you can relax and enjoy the scenery. (If you have time, I highly recommend the side trip down Saints John Trail. You must turn around at the bottom.) Descend moderate Deer Creek Trail and loop back towards Webster Pass and Radical Hill. A tough rocky spot at the bottom of Radical Hill is followed by an attention-getting shelf road near the top.

Other nearby routes: Peru Creek, Trail #18, is passed on way to alternate starting point near Montezuma. From Webster Pass, you can descend Handcart Gulch and return via daunting Red Cone, Trail #20.

Services: Full services in Breckenridge. Porta-potty in Montezuma.

Directions: *(Shadowed portion of trail is described here.)*

WP	Mile	Action
01	0.0	N39° 31.30´ W105° 57.57´ Continue southeast on Tiger Road.
02	0.9	N39° 30.79´ W105° 56.82´ Turn left before bridge.
	1.5	Road curves right past large camp spot and enters trees at seasonal gate marked F.S. 221.
03	2.7	N39° 31.43´ W105° 55.26´ Main road switchbacks uphill to left. Continue straight on rougher road.
04	3.2	N39° 31.63´ W105° 54.80´ Turn hard right at dilapidated cabins, cross stream and begin steep, rough climb up Garibaldi Gulch.
	4.7	"T" intersection above timberline. Turn left to continue, but first make short trip right to Wise Mountain.
	5.5	Climb extremely steep, rocky hill to great views.
05	6.8/0.0	N39° 31.38´ W105° 52.92´ Continue straight. (Left here is Saints John, a great side trip with lots to see.)
06	0.8	N39° 31.25´ W105° 52.14´ Turn left at "T."
	1.3	Stay left downhill on Deer Creek, then stay right as several roads join on left.
07	4.6	N39° 33.85´ W105° 51.62´ Parking lot for alternate starting point. Continue downhill.
	4.9/0.0	Turn right towards Webster Pass. (Public road crosses private property.)
	0.4	Stay right, then avoid private roads branching off.

WP	Mile	Action
	0.6	Forest gate. F.S. 285 starts here.
	1.4	Road curves right and crosses creek. Continue uphill.
08	2.6	N39° 32.30´ W105° 50.50´ Continue straight to Webster Pass.
	3.8	Webster Pass. Turn around and return to Waypoint 08.
08	5.0/0.0	Turn left for Radical Hill on F.S. 286.
	1.9	Top of Radical Hill. Road curves left to Deer Creek.
	2.8	Stay left and return to Waypoint 06.
06	3.3	Continue straight on F.S. 5 to Middle Fork of Swan.
09	4.0/0.0	N39° 30.81´ W105° 51.75´ Turn right downhill on Middle Fork of the Swan River, marked F.S. 6. (Option: Continue straight to overlook and hiking trail.)
	0.7	Stay on best road down very steep section.
	2.2	Historic Swandyke Cabin on right.
10	2.9	N39° 30.16´ W105° 54.07´ Stay right. Road to left goes up extremely difficult hill to Glacier Ridge.
	5.6	Swing right on F.S. 6 after seasonal gate.
	6.3	Continue straight (north) on Tiger Road.
01	7.7	Return to start.

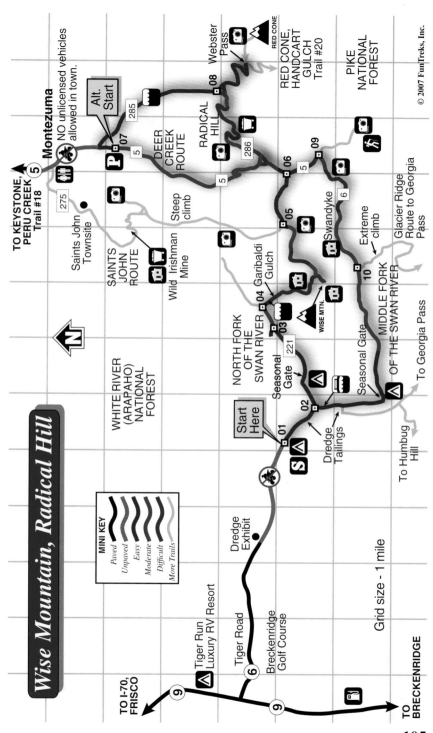

Wise Mountain, Radical Hill

MINI KEY

Paved
Unpaved
Easy
Moderate
Difficult
More Trails

Grid size - 1 mile

TO I-70, FRISCO

Tiger Run Luxury RV Resort

Tiger Road

Breckenridge Golf Course

Dredge Exhibit

TO BRECKENRIDGE

Start Here

01

02

Dredge Tailings

Seasonal Gate

Seasonal Gate

To Humbug Hill

To Georgia Pass

NORTH FORK OF THE SWAN RIVER

WHITE RIVER (ARAPAHO) NATIONAL FOREST

Saints John Townsite

SAINTS JOHN ROUTE

Wild Irishman Mine

Steep climb

Montezuma

TO KEYSTONE, PERU CREEK Trail #18

NO unlicensed vehicles allowed in town.

Alt. Start

07

285

5

5

5

DEER CREEK ROUTE

RADICAL HILL

08

286

Webster Pass

RED CONE, HANDCART GULCH Trail #20

RED CONE

PIKE NATIONAL FOREST

09

06

05

04 Garibaldi Gulch

03

221

WISE MTN.

Swandyke

6

5

10

Extreme climb

Glacier Ridge Route to Georgia Pass

MIDDLE FORK OF THE SWAN RIVER

To Georgia Pass

6

9

9

© 2007 FunTreks, Inc.

105

Hall Valley Campground fills up quickly on Labor Day weekend.

Author above Handcart Gulch at Webster Pass.

Red Cone climb is tough.

Looking down on Webster Pass from top of Red Cone.

Below timberline.

Point of no return starts at 12,800 ft. elevation.

Little Rascal Hill.

Red Cone, Handcart Gulch

20

Getting There: Take Highway 285 southwest from Denver about 42 miles from the 470 outerbelt. Turn right on C.R. 60 about 3 miles after Grant. Continue 4.5 miles to staging area on left.

Staging/Camping: Staging area is fairly large but fills up quickly on busy summer weekends. Just ahead are Handcart Gulch and Hall Valley Forest Service Campgrounds. Many excellent dispersed camping spots along the Hall Valley route.

Difficulty: Hall Valley is easy, Handcart Gulch is moderate and Red Cone is difficult. The one-way descent from Red Cone to Webster Pass is extremely steep and potentially dangerous. Make sure brakes on all four wheels are working properly. Even with adequate brakes, you will slide on the steepest sections. Allow wheels to turn slightly to maintain steering control. You may have to apply a little throttle to avoid getting sideways on the hill. Don't go down this section if Webster Pass is snow covered. You can't get back up. Snow can block the south side of Webster Pass well into mid summer. (See page 15 for carburetor adj.)

Highlights: Incredible views from Red Cone looking down to Webster Pass and Radical Hill in the distance. An extreme thrill ride coming down one-way section from Red Cone. When clear of snow, you can reach Webster Pass by going up Handcart Gulch.

Time & Distance: The loop up Red Cone and down Handcart Gulch is 11.9 miles and takes 3 to 4 hours. Hall Valley is 4.2 miles one way.

Trail Description: Continue uphill from staging area. Trail soon forks with Handcart Gulch to left and Red Cone to right. To avoid difficult one-way descent from Red Cone, ride each trail in both directions. The route up to Red Cone is very steep and rocky and should not be attempted by novice riders. Handcart Gulch is a very pleasant ride with interesting features along the way. Hall Valley ends in a scenic valley where you must turn around.

Other nearby route: From Webster Pass, you can connect with Wise Mountain/Radical Hill, Trail #19.

Services: Full services in Conifer. Other gas stations along 285.

Directions: *(Shadowed portion of trail is described here.)*

WP	Mile	Action
01	0.0	N39° 28.92´ W105° 47.60´ Head west.
	0.6	Stay right on 120 and weave up-hill through area where cars may be parked. (Hall Valley 120B is left.)
02	0.7/0.0	N39° 29.04´ W105° 48.29´ Rocky road forks. Right is Red Cone 565; left is Handcart Gulch 121.
02	0.0	LOOP ROUTE UP RED CONE Stay right. Road gets rockier.
	0.2	Stay right. Road becomes very steep and rocky as it climbs through trees. (Left on 565.2 is another way to reach Handcart Gulch.)
	3.0	Trail climbs above timberline. Little Rascal Hill can be seen ahead.
03	5.6	N39° 31.61´ W105° 49.34´ Top of Red Cone and point of no return. First descent is **not** the steepest.

WP	Mile	Action
04	6.3/0.0	N39° 31.88´ W105° 49.95´ Webster Pass. Stay left on narrow shelf road to descend Handcart Gulch.
	4.5	Stay right on F.S. 121. (565.2 goes left back to Red Cone.)
02	4.9/0.0	Loop complete. Stay right to return to staging area and Hall Valley route.
02	0.0	ROUTE UP HANDCART GULCH Stay left on rocky road 121.
	0.4	Stay left. (565.2 goes right to Red Cone.)
	1.7	Bear left around dilapidated miner's cabin. Private, keep out.
	2.4	Pass through repaired mud bog.
	3.0	Pass through area of mine tailings and begin climb up narrow switchbacks.
04	4.9	N39° 31.88´ W105° 49.95´ Arrive at Webster Pass.

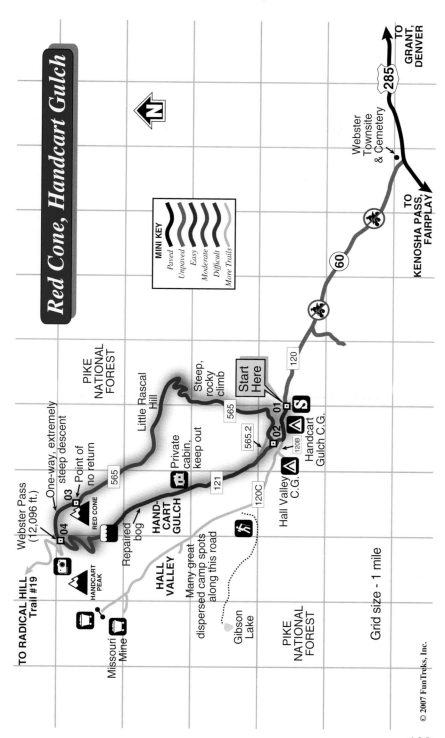

Red Cone, Handcart Gulch

N

MINI KEY
Paved
Unpaved
Easy
Moderate
Difficult
More Trails

TO
GRANT,
DENVER

285

Webster
Townsite
& Cemetery

TO
KENOSHA PASS,
FAIRPLAY

60

120

Start
Here

Steep,
rocky
climb

565

01

S

02

565.2

120B

Handcart
Gulch C.G.

PIKE
NATIONAL
FOREST

Little Rascal
Hill

Private cabin,
keep out

121

Hall Valley
C.G.

120C

Many great
dispersed camp spots
along this road

HALL
VALLEY

HAND-
CART
GULCH

Gibson
Lake

PIKE
NATIONAL
FOREST

Grid size - 1 mile

One-way, extremely
steep descent

Point of
no return

Webster Pass
(12,096 ft.)

03

565

RED CONE

04

Repaired
bog

TO RADICAL HILL
Trail #19

HANDCART
PEAK

Missouri
Mine

Climb up McCallister Gulch begins here.

View of Camp Hale from Hornsilver Mtn.

Descending Hornsilver Mountain.

Stop and shut off engine around horses.

Steep obstacle on Lime Creek Road.

Benson Cabin marks start of tough trail.

One of several views of Mt. Holy Cross.

Side trip on 757 along Pearl Creek.

Wildflower patch along Wearyman Creek.

110

Camp Hale Area

21

Getting There: **From Leadville:** Take Hwy. 24 north from Leadville about 17 miles to the north end of Camp Hale. Turn right 0.4 miles north of mile marker 159. **From Vail:** Head west on Interstate 70 to Exit 171. Head south on Hwy. 24 about 15 miles and turn left into Camp Hale 0.6 miles south of mile marker 158.

Staging/Camping: Unload and camp at many great spots adjacent to roads that crisscross Camp Hale. Follow F.S. 702 to starting point shown on map. Large shaded camp spots can be found on 702 north of start. Developed fee camping at south end of Camp Hale.

Difficulty: Most of these trails are easy to moderate. Two difficult spots, however, need special mention because they can't be bypassed. One is at the top of McCallister Gulch; the other is near the beginning of Lime Creek. The climb to Resolution Mountain is optional, as is the very difficult Benson Cabin route.

Highlights: A wide variety of twisting roads perfect for ATVs. Most routes are between 9,000 and 11,000 feet; however, a few places, like Resolution Mountain, approach 12,000 ft. Distant views of Mt. Holy Cross and great seasonal wildflowers. A popular hiking and horseback riding area. Please stop and shut off your engine around horses.

Time & Distance: The combined distance of the two adjoining loops is 42 miles. Take your time and enjoy a full day of riding. Take a second day and ride in reverse direction for a completely different experience.

Trail Description: Climb steeply through dense forest to Resolution Mountain, then descend back down to multiple crossings of Wearyman Creek. Climb steep, rocky Lime Creek Road and return via easy but beautiful Shrine Pass Road. Finish with final climb up Wearyman Creek to Ptarmigan Pass and return via easy Resolution Road.

Other nearby route: Red & White Mountain, Trail #17, is located north of I-70 at Vail.

Services: Full services in Leadville and Vail. Gas and food in Minturn. Guided ATV Tours and rentals available by reservation at Nova Guides, Inc. (See map for location and appendix for contact information.)

Directions: *(Shadowed portion of trail is described here.)*

WP	Mile	Action
01	**0.0**	*N39° 26.88 W106° 19.15´* Head north on F.S. 708 from starting point shown on map.
	0.8	Turn right at T after passing by camp spots in trees.
	1.2	Turn right uphill at sign for 708 and follow shelf road to left. Stay right uphill past private residence.
	4.1	Road swings right and gets very steep. Be careful.
	4.6	Trail turns left out of trees. Great views to right.
	5.0	Turn right up steep climb to Resolution Mountain.
	5.6/0.0	Return to main trail and continue to right.
02	**5.5**	*N39° 31.21 W106° 18.86´* At bottom of mountain, intersect with Wearyman Creek. Turn left and cross creek several times.
03	**6.2**	*N39° 31.39 W106° 19.54´* After bridge, turn left on Shrine Pass Road 709.
04	**6.8/0.0**	*N39° 31.39 W106° 20.19´* Turn right at information board to begin Lime Creek Road.
	0.5	Climb difficult rocky spot, then continue uphill on narrow road until road swings right across meadow.
05	**4.0**	*N39° 33.83 W106° 18.43´* After steep spot out of meadow, turn left on good road. Right is closed.
	4.3	Continue straight on better road F.S. 728.
06	**9.4/0.0**	*N39° 33.62´ W106° 15.51´* Turn right on Shrine Pass Road. (Option: Go left first for scenic ride.)
07	**3.2/0.0**	*N39° 32.44´ W106° 18.30´* Difficult Benson Cabin route goes left. Round trip adds 4 miles.
03	**1.7**	Turn left across bridge back to Wearyman Creek.
02	**2.4/0.0**	Return to Waypoint 02. Turn left on 747. After several more stream crossings, narrow shelf road winds its way to Ptarmigan Pass.
08	**5.0**	*N39° 29.58´ W106° 15.20´* Ptarmigan Pass. Continue down other side on easy Resolution Road.
09	**9.1**	*N39° 27.61´ W106° 17.97´* Continue straight. (Option: Turn left on 715, then quickly turn left to explore difficult Pearl Creek 757.)
01	**10.5**	Pass through seasonal gate back to start.

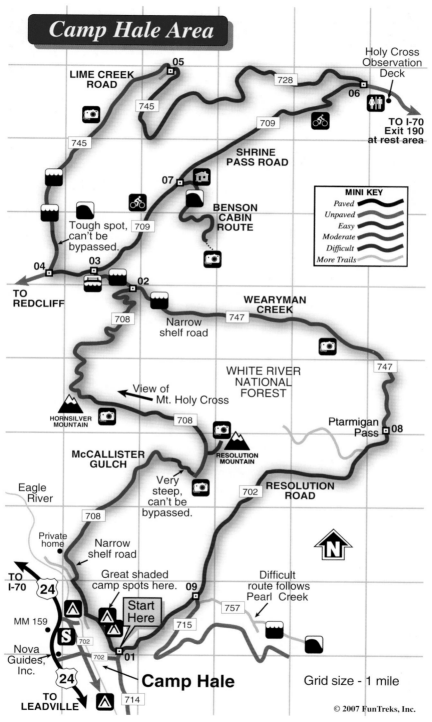

Camp Hale Area

LIME CREEK ROAD

05

745

745

728

Holy Cross Observation Deck

06

TO I-70 Exit 190 at rest area

709

SHRINE PASS ROAD

07

BENSON CABIN ROUTE

709

Tough spot, can't be bypassed.

MINI KEY
Paved
Unpaved
Easy
Moderate
Difficult
More Trails

04

03

02

TO REDCLIFF

708

Narrow shelf road

747

WEARYMAN CREEK

747

WHITE RIVER NATIONAL FOREST

View of Mt. Holy Cross

708

HORNSILVER MOUNTAIN

Ptarmigan Pass

08

McCALLISTER GULCH

RESOLUTION MOUNTAIN

Very steep, can't be bypassed.

702

RESOLUTION ROAD

Eagle River

708

Private home

TO I-70 24

Narrow shelf road

MM 159

Great shaded camp spots here.

Start Here

09

715

Difficult route follows Pearl Creek

757

N

S

702

Nova Guides, Inc.

702

01

24

Camp Hale

Grid size - 1 mile

TO LEADVILLE

714

© 2007 FunTreks, Inc.

113

First staging area along Rampart Range Road.

Start of Overlook Trail #682.

Great fun and lots of challenges.

Travel with a friend and wear a helmet.

Many hills and banked curves.

High scenic viewpoints along the way.

Sprucewood Inn, popular restaurant and bar.

Dirt bikers pause at Kips Bridge.

Rampart Range OHV Area 22

Getting There: From Denver, take Hwy. 85 south to Sedalia. Turn west on Hwy. 67 and go about 10 miles to Rampart Range Road on left.

Staging/Camping: As you head south on Rampart Range Road, go short distance past parking area on left to first staging area on right. Camping spots and many more staging areas follow. All connect to Trail #690 that runs parallel to Rampart Road. To reach Flat Rocks Campground, continue 4.2 miles on washboard road and turn right.

Difficulty: Trails selected here are at the high end of moderate. Novice riders may find some spots difficult. All trails are narrow with two-way traffic and very crowded on weekends. When possible, ride during the week or early in the day on weekends. Slow down for blind curves. Always use hand signals to indicate number of riders behind you. ATVs should stay off single-track routes. No unlicensed vehicles are allowed on Rampart Range Road in the summer. Avoid riding in the spring when roads are muddy. Always wear an approved helmet.

Highlights: The routes shown here are only a small sample of the many miles of trails in the area. Route-finding can be confusing. The best detailed map of the area is published by the Rampart Range Motorcycle Management Committee. (To obtain, see "Services" below.)

Time & Distance: The route shown here is 32.4 miles. Allow 5 to 6 hours. Add at least an hour to visit Sprucewood Inn via Trail #673.

Trail Description: Scotts Trail, #681, crosses tippy rock slabs. The north end of Tomahawk Trail, #685, is just barely wide enough for a large ATV as it winds through tight trees. Trail #674 is steep and rocky as it climbs east after crossing Pine Creek. Trail #673, which heads north to Sprucewood Inn, is very twisty with many banked turns. Take your time on this road to avoid accidents.

Other nearby route: Rainbow Falls OHV Area, Trail #23, is just south of Rampart Range OHV Area. Trail #650 connects the two areas.

Services: Gas and supplies in Sedalia. Food, supplies and maps available at Bugling Bull Trading Post, 1 mile east of Rampart Range Road on Hwy. 67. Sprucewood Inn, a restaurant and bar, also sells the Rampart map. The Inn is located 3 miles past Rampart Range Road on 67.

115

Directions: *(Shadowed portion of trail is described here.)*

WP	Mile	Action
01	**0.0**	*N39° 22.61 W105° 05.69´* Head south on 690 parallel to Rampart Road. Stay left for easier route.
	4.1	After parking area, turn left on road that goes to Flat Rocks Campground. Cross Rampart Road and bear right to start of Overlook Trail 682.
02	**4.1/0.0**	*N39° 19.62 W105° 05.20´* Head east.
	0.6	After overlook, 682 goes both ways. Stay right.
	1.1	Stay right on 682 where 683 intersects.
	2.5	Continue straight where 646 goes left.
03	**2.8**	*N39° 18.41 W105° 04.96´* Cross gravel road 502. Stay left, then left again at next fork.
	4.0	After crossing slanted rock slab, bear left.
	4.4	Stay right where 646 goes left.
04	**4.9/0.0**	*N39° 18.93 W105° 03.94´* Cross gravel road 502 to start of Tomahawk Trail 685.
	2.0	After narrow downhill section, cross Kips Bridge.
	3.4	Stay left on 686 then stay right at next two forks.
05	**4.7**	*N39° 20.43 W105° 04.86´* Cross Rampart Range Road 300, then head south on 690.
	6.0/0.0	Return to parking area and continue south on 690.
06	**2.9**	*N39° 17.63´ W105° 05.54´* Weave through confusing intersection of roads to head west on 657.
	3.9	Stay right on 657 where 680 goes left.
	5.8	Stay right on 675.
07	**8.7**	*N39° 19.14´ W105° 07.36´* Turn right on 674.
	10.3	Cross creek. Begin climb.
	10.9	Stay right on 674 where road shortcuts left to 673.
08	**12.6**	*N39° 19.82´ W105° 05.74´* Bear right, then right again at next fork to return to parking lot. (Option: Left at Waypoint 08 goes to Sprucewood Inn. Take 673 north about 3 miles.)
	13.3	Back to parking lot. If you started at Waypoint 01, head north on 690 to return to start.
01	**17.4**	Back to staging area at Waypoint 01.

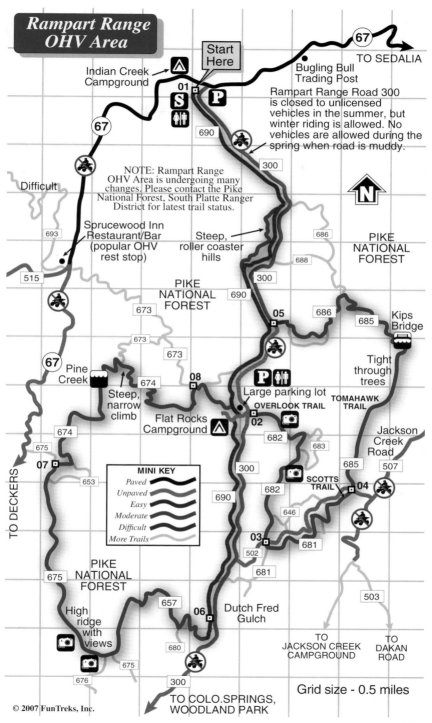

Rampart Range OHV Area

Indian Creek Campground

Start Here

01

690

TO SEDALIA

67

Bugling Bull Trading Post

Rampart Range Road 300 is closed to unlicensed vehicles in the summer, but winter riding is allowed. No vehicles are allowed during the spring when road is muddy.

300

Difficult

693

NOTE: Rampart Range OHV Area is undergoing many changes. Please contact the Pike National Forest, South Platte Ranger District for latest trail status.

N

Sprucewood Inn Restaurant/Bar (popular OHV rest stop)

Steep, roller coaster hills

686

PIKE NATIONAL FOREST

515

688

PIKE NATIONAL FOREST

300

690

673

05

686

685

Kips Bridge

673

673

Tight through trees

67

Pine Creek

Steep, narrow climb

674

08

P

Large parking lot

TOMAHAWK TRAIL

674

Flat Rocks Campground

OVERLOOK TRAIL

02

682

Jackson Creek Road

675

683

685

507

07

653

MINI KEY
Paved
Unpaved
Easy
Moderate
Difficult
More Trails

300

682

SCOTTS TRAIL

04

690

646

PIKE NATIONAL FOREST

675

03

681

502

503

681

657

06

Dutch Fred Gulch

High ridge with views

680

TO JACKSON CREEK CAMPGROUND

TO DAKAN ROAD

675

300

676

TO COLO.SPRINGS, WOODLAND PARK

Grid size - 0.5 miles

TO DECKERS

Large staging area can accommodate many vehicles.

Ruts and washouts can increase difficulty.

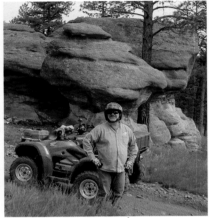
Rock outcrop on western loop.

Wildflowers revive burn area.

Hayman burn area in distance.

118

Rainbow Falls OHV Area

Getting There: From Woodland Park, head north on Highway 67 about 10 miles. Turn right at large sign for Rainbow Falls three miles after Manitou Lake. Drive east 0.2 miles and turn right to large staging area.

Staging/Camping: Unload at staging area or, if camping, drive in a mile or so on F.S. 348 or 350 where you'll find great camp spots. Also, note South Meadows F.S. Campground along Highway 67.

Difficulty: Eastern loop is mostly moderate. Western loop is easy. Unexpected washouts on steep sections can increase difficulty. Secondary trails, like 634, 347C and others, can be very difficult. A detailed OHV map of the area is available from the Forest Service and at the ATV dealer on Main Street in Woodland Park.

Highlights: This is a very popular OHV area with many miles of challenging and scenic trails. Only a portion are described here. Unfortunately, the area has been subject to a great deal of abuse. It is critical that you ride on marked trails at all times. Pack out your trash and pick up after others whenever possible. Report violators.

Time & Distance: Eastern loop is 10.8 miles. Western Loop is 7.8 miles. Allow a half day. Explore other routes for full day or weekend.

Trail Description: Eastern loop meanders through a variety of terrain reaching higher elevations along the west side of Rampart Range. Some of the trails are quite steep. Routes are fairly well marked. The western loop is relatively flat as it skirts through parts of the Hayman burn area. It's a great place for novice riders to explore. Recovery of the area can be seen in the form of new seasonal wildflowers, abundant along the trails.

Other nearby route: Just north of Rainbow Falls is the Rampart Range OHV Area. Licensed vehicles can get there by heading north on Long Hollow Road 348 to Rampart Range Road 300, then turning left. Unlicensed vehicles must use connecting Trail 650, which is not shown on map. To find 650, continue north on 348 about a mile past forest gate just off northern edge of map. Trail is on left.

Services: Full services in Woodland Park. Manitou Lake has toilets.

Directions: (*Shadowed portion of trail is described here.*)

WP	Mile	Action
01	0.0	EASTERN LOOP N39° 08.16´ W105° 06.39´ From staging area, return to 350 and head north.
02	1.0	N39° 08.99´ W105°06.64´ Turn right on 350A. Climb through camping area as road gets rougher.
	2.2	Continue straight. 350B joins on left.
03	2.6/0.0	N39° 09.46´ W105° 05.48´ Turn right on Long Hollow Road 348. (Option: Explore more difficult trails to left.)
	0.6	Make hard right where 347 goes north.
04	0.7	N39° 09.12´ W105° 05.15´ Turn left uphill on rougher 348C.
	2.0	Turn right on easier 347.
05	3.0/0.0	N39° 09.23´ W105° 03.97´ Hard right turn on 344. (Option: Explore trails to left.)
	0.6	Turn right to overlook, then return and continue downhill on 344.
	1.0	After steep hill, stay left.
06	1.3	N39° 08.83´ W105° 04.63´ Turn right on 348A.
	1.9	Bear right and follow loop back uphill to 344. This section is very steep.

WP	Mile	Action
	2.6	At top of hill, turn right on 344.
06	2.7	At Wpt. 06 again. This time, bear left.
	3.4	Stay right as roads converge. (Left loops around steep rock obstacle.)
	3.5	Continue right downhill on 344.
	4.6	Stay right.
07	4.8	N39° 08.23´ W105° 06.23´ Turn left on 348.
01	5.2/0.0	Return to staging area.
		WESTERN LOOP
01	0.0	Turn left on 350 towards Hwy. 67.
	0.2	Turn right through gate. Close it and next gate.
08	1.5	N39° 08.87´ W105° 07.29´ Turn left at T.
09	2.8	N39° 09.45´ W105° 08.12´ Right on 332C.
	3.4	Stay right heading south.
	3.6	Stay right. (Option: Side trip left to overlook.)
10	4.6	N39° 09.40´ W105° 07.28´ Left uphill on 332A.
	5.7	Left on 332B. Go by rock outcrop.
08	6.1	Turn left and go out the way you came in.

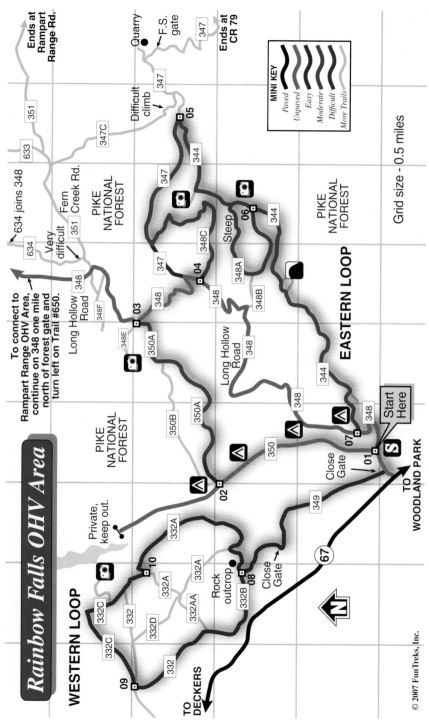

Rainbow Falls OHV Area

MINI KEY
- Paved
- Unpaved
- Easy
- Moderate
- Difficult
- More Trails

Grid size - 0.5 miles

WESTERN LOOP

EASTERN LOOP

PIKE NATIONAL FOREST

PIKE NATIONAL FOREST

PIKE NATIONAL FOREST

Ends at Rampart Range Rd.

Ends at CR 79

Quarry

F.S. gate

Difficult climb

Very difficult

634 joins 348

To connect to Rampart Range OHV Area, continue on 348 one mile north of forest gate and turn left on Trail #650.

Fern Creek Rd.

Long Hollow Road

Long Hollow Road

Steep

Private, keep out.

Rock outcrop

Close Gate

Close Gate

Start Here

TO WOODLAND PARK

TO DECKERS

N

351
633
634
347C
347
347
347
344
351
351
348
348F
348E
350A
350A
350B
348
347
348C
04
348
348
348A
348B
06
344
344
344
348
350
349
350
332A
332A
332A
332AA
332B
332
332D
332C
332C
332
332
05
03
02
01
07
08
09
10
S

© 2007 FunTreks, Inc.

121

Trail description starts here near Woodland Park.

Approaching open area near Waypoint 02.

Fantastic roller-coaster terrain.

View of Pikes Peak from Phantom Creek Road.

Tight squeeze between boulders.

Many camp spots along 363, 362 and north 357.

Careful crossing this bridge.

North Divide 717 OHV Area ◆24◆

Getting There: From Woodland Park, drive west on Highway 24 about 1 mile and turn right on County Road 25 at traffic light. See map for directions to alternate starting points.

Staging/Camping: Mileages are reset at alternate starting points making it possible to start from different points around the loop. Consider the pros and cons of each. The largest staging area and best camping is on Phantom Creek Road 363. You can also camp on F.S. 357 west of Painted Rocks F.S. Campground; however, this section is in the Hayman burn area. Trails do not directly connect to Painted Rocks C.G.

Difficulty: The route described here is a mix of easy, moderate and difficult trails. The toughest section is at the north end of 717A before Waypoint 03. Novice riders should bypass this section by heading west on 357A at Waypoint 02, then heading north on easy 357. Route finding is extremely challenging. A detailed map of the area is available from the Forest Service or at the ATV dealer in Woodland Park.

Highlights: The map shown here covers the southern half of the OHV area, most of which was not affected by the Hayman Fire. The trails are fun and the scenery is great. It would take several days of hard riding to cover all the trails in the area.

Time & Distance: As described here, the trail measures 43.4 miles and takes 4 to 6 hours depending on riding skills.

Trail Description: Entering the area via 717A is the closest starting point to Woodland Park, but it is also the most difficult entry route. If you're up to the challenge, however, you'll find the ride extremely enjoyable. A variety of surprises continue along the route. Trail 717C is an easier alternative to 717B. After you've ridden what's described here, return to explore side roads and the northern part of OHV area.

Other nearby route: Rainbow Falls OHV Area, Trail #23, is located northeast of this area on Highway 67. An advantage to camping on the north end of 357 is that this area is very close to Rainbow Falls.

Services: Full services in Woodland Park. Gas and a small shopping center in Divide. No services on trails.

Directions: *(Shadowed portion of trail is described here.)*

WP	Mile	Action
01	0.0	N38° 58.91´ W105° 06.37´ Head north from staging area on 717A.
	0.6	Turn right on 356, then left on 717A.
	2.7	Left across creek, then driver's choice up steep hill.
	3.4	Right on better traveled road.
	4.1	Continue on F.S. 354.
	5.0	Open area, stay right, cross stream.
02	5.3	N39° 01.42´ W105° 07.78´ FS 717A goes both ways. Stay right then north. (Don't go up steep hill to left.)
	5.5	Cross narrow wooden bridge.
	6.2	Right on 357B short distance, then left through posts for 717A.
	6.7	Straight at 4-way intersection.
	7.3	Descend difficult rocky spot.
	8.9	After winding, narrow trail, go straight at 4-way intersection.
03	9.2/0.0	N39° 02.93´ W105° 08.71´ Reach 357. Look for 717A across road. May be north.
	0.8	Open area after steep descent. Cross 364, then stay left uphill on 717A.
	1.3	Turn left on 717.
	2.2	Continue straight on 717.
	2.4	Better road. Take left, then quick right.
	3.6	Bear left on better road 355.
04	4.0	N39° 00.73´ W105° 10.40´ Bear right through posts on 717.
	5.0	Cross creek at boulders and turn left.
	5.3	Squeeze between giant boulders.
	5.5	Stay right at distinctive rock.
	5.6	Turn right downhill and cross creek.
	6.3	Continue straight across road.
	6.9	Cross creek, bear right in gulch.
	7.7	Bear right after creek.
	8.4	Turn right. Trail joins on left.
	10.3	Turn right on Yucca Valley Road.
	10.4	Turn left off Yucca Valley Road.
	12.3	Turn left where 717C goes right.
	12.4	Turn right. (Straight goes to 363.)
05	12.6/0.0	N39° 01.47´ W105° 14.69´ Turn right on 717B. (Left goes to alternate staging area on 363.)
	0.4	Stay right.
	2.7	Cross very narrow bridge, then stay right through winding, steep spot.
	3.0	Continue straight past bridge.
06	3.8/0.0	N39° 02.51´ W105° 12.43´ Climb long hill to Phantom Creek Road. Cross road and continue on 717B.
	2.0	After creek, bear right at next 3 forks.
07	3.0	N39° 04.01´ W105° 10.93´ Connect with 364. Go straight short distance, then turn right on 363.
	3.8	Pass through gate, stay right on 363.
	4.7	Rock outcrop on left with view.
08	5.1/0.0	N39° 03.10´ W105° 11.65´ Turn left downhill on winding 363B.
	1.3	Turn left. Stay south on 355.
09	4.6/0.0	N39° 00.64´ W105° 09.91´ Turn left on 357. Go northeast past 364.
10	1.8/0.0	N39° 01.32´ W105° 08.65´ Turn right off 357 at nice camp spot on left, then bear left on 357A. This road heads downhill on an amazing roller-coaster ride. When you reach creek at bottom, bear left. Take shortcut over steep hump to return to 717A.
	1.3	Stay right after going over hump and follow 717A to right downhill the way you came up.
01	6.3	Return to parking lot at starting point.

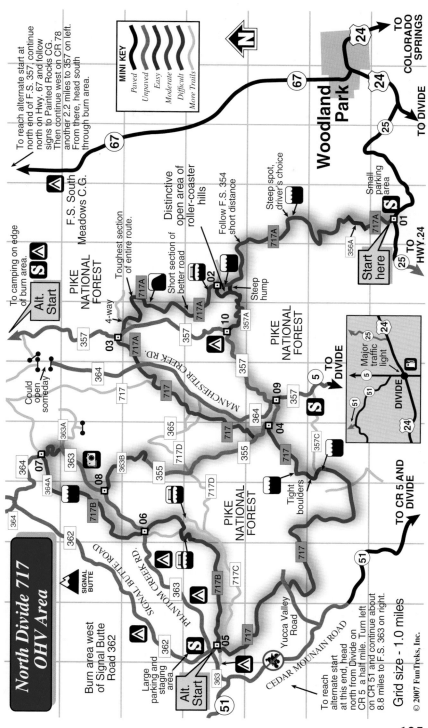

North Divide 717 OHV Area

MINI KEY
Paved
Unpaved
Easy
Moderate
Difficult
More Trails

N

TO COLORADO SPRINGS

TO DIVIDE

TO HWY. 24

Woodland Park

To reach alternate start at north end of F.S. 357, continue north on Hwy. 67 and follow signs to Painted Rocks CG. Then continue west on CR 78 another 2.2 miles to 357 on left. From there, head south through burn area.

F.S. South Meadows C.G.

To camping on edge of burn area.

Alt. Start

PIKE NATIONAL FOREST

Toughest section of entire route.

4-way

Short section of better road

Distinctive open area of roller-coaster hills

Follow F.S. 354 short distance

Steep hump

Steep spot, driver's choice

Small parking area

Start here

PIKE NATIONAL FOREST

TO DIVIDE

Major traffic light

DIVIDE

Could open someday

MANCHESTER CREEK RD.

Tight boulders

PIKE NATIONAL FOREST

TO CR 5 AND DIVIDE

SIGNAL BUTTE

Burn area west of Signal Butte Road 362

Large parking and staging area

Alt. Start

PHANTOM CREEK RD.

SIGNAL BUTTE ROAD

Yucca Valley Road

CEDAR MOUNTAIN ROAD

To reach alternate start at this end, head north from Divide on CR 5 a half mile. Turn left on CR 51 and continue about 8.8 miles to F.S. 363 on right.

Grid size - 1.0 miles

© 2007 FunTreks, Inc.

125

Great camp spots with views atop Shields Gulch 315. Use alternate start off Hwy. 24.

Don't ride without a helmet.

Difficult spot on Trail #6029.

ATV trails are well marked.

Damage from heavy rains.

Beautiful view across valley to Collegiate Peaks.

Fourmile North

Getting There: From center of Buena Vista, turn east on Main Street at traffic light. Cross railroad tracks, go another block and turn left on North Colorado Avenue. Head north 2.7 miles to F.S. 375 on right before tunnels. Alternate starting point is east of Johnson Village on Hwy. 24/285. Go east 4.8 miles past Arkansas River. Look for 315 on left.

Staging/Camping: Main staging area is large with plenty of room to park. Information board usually has detailed maps of area; check dispenser. You'll find great dispersed camp spots along 375 and first part of 376. No room to park at alternate start. Drive in 2 miles for scenic camping and staging on left. Sandy F.S. 315 is usually hard packed and suitable for motorhomes; however, heavy storms can make the road impassable on rare occasions. Check conditions before entering.

Difficulty: Route selected here is easy so that all skill levels can enjoy the beauty of the area. Those looking for more challenge can find it on marked ATV trails that branch off. The toughest trail is #6029. It is extremely steep in spots with one very tight squeeze between boulders. Most other side trails are manageable for riders with basic skills. Trail #1414 has a few minor challenges but is still easy.

Highlights: Trails meander along a high ridge east of Buena Vista with stunning views of the Collegiate Peaks in distance. Because of sandy soil, the trails are always changing due to erosion and repacking. This results in twisting and undulating terrain that is fun to ride and usually not difficult. It is absolutely critical that you stay on existing trails.

Time & Distance: The basic route described here is about 27 miles and takes 2 to 3 hours. Allow a full day to cover the entire north side.

Trail Description: The trail heads east then circles around large loop to return via same route. This allows an opportunity to try side trails in either direction. Riders of different abilities can split up, then rejoin.

Other nearby routes: Fourmile South, Trail #26, is just south of Hwy. 24. Four great mountain trails in Collegiate Peaks across valley.

Services: Gas and food at Johnson Village. Full services in Buena Vista. KOA campground off Hwy. 24 east of Johnson Village.

Directions: *(Shadowed portion of trail is described here.)*

WP	Mile	Action
01	0.0	*N38° 52.47´ W106° 08.67´* Head uphill from staging area on wide gravel road 375.
	0.5	Continue straight. (West end of optional ATV Trail #6037 on right.)
02	1.1	*N38° 53.06´ W106° 08.45´* Turn right on 376.
	1.3	Continue straight. (Great camp spots on right and access to Trail #6038.)
	1.6	Continue straight. (East end of Trail #6037 on right.)
	1.7	Continue straight. (Trail #1415 goes left.)
	2.0	Continue straight across Fourmile Creek.
	2.2	Continue straight. (Difficult #6029 on right.)
	2.3	Continue straight. (West end of #6039 on right.)
	2.5	Turn right out of wash. (Private road goes left.)
03	3.0/0.0	*N38° 52.65´ W106° 06.66´* Roads converge at opening in fence. Turn left before fence on 311.
	0.5	Stay right on 311 where 373 goes left.
04	1.4	*N38° 53.36´ W106° 05.75´* Continue straight. (Trail #1414 goes right. This fun and scenic ride is suitable for novice riders, but all skill levels will enjoy it.)

WP	Mile	Action
05	2.4/0.0	*N38° 54.10´ W106° 05.38´* Turn left on 373. (Right on 311 goes to other end of Trail 1414. Beyond is Trout Creek Pass at Hwy. 24 in another 7 miles.)
06	1.5	*N38° 54.80´ W106° 06.59´* Bear left on 373 at triangular intersection. (Right on 373A dead ends in short distance at Davis Meadow Hiking Trail.)
07	3.9	*N38° 53.27´ W106° 06.63´* Turn left uphill out of sandy wash on 373. (Right on 375A goes to F.S 375, where a left turn takes you back to staging area.)
	4.4	Turn right on 311.
03	4.9/0.0	Back to Waypoint 03. Turn left on fun ride up Lenhardy Cutoff route 376.
08	4.2	*N38° 51.49´ W106° 03.24´* Turn right on 315. As you descend Shields Gulch, roads to right goes to great camp spots with views.
09	6.8	*N38° 50.10´ W106° 01.37´* Alternate start at Hwy. 24
09	0.0	DIRECTIONS FROM ALTERNATE START Head north uphill on 315. (This sandy road occasionally gets washed out. If packed and dry, it is usually suitable for campers and motor homes.)
	1.8	After hill, roads go left to great camp spots.
08	2.6	Turn left down F.S. 376 to roads already described.

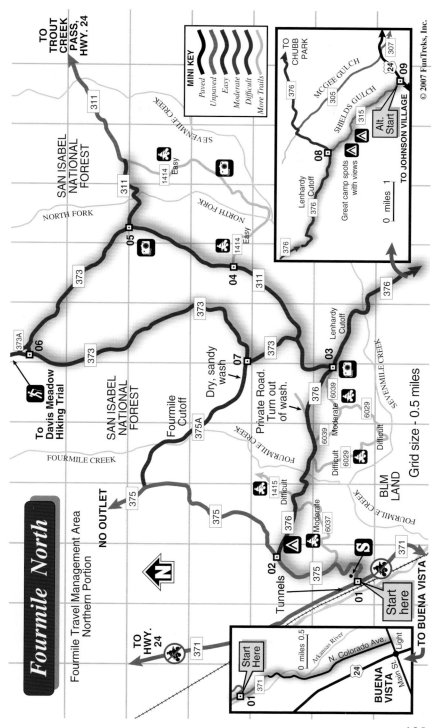

Fourmile North

Fourmile Travel Management Area
Northern Portion

NO OUTLET

N

Grid size - 0.5 miles

MINI KEY

Paved
Unpaved
Easy
Moderate
Difficult
More Trails

© 2007 FunTreks, Inc.

TO TROUT CREEK PASS, HWY. 24

SAN ISABEL NATIONAL FOREST

NORTH FORK

NORTH FORK

SEVENMILE CREEK

311

311

311

311

373

373

373

373

373A

06

05

04

1414 Easy

1414 Easy

To Davis Meadow Hiking Trail

SAN ISABEL NATIONAL FOREST

FOURMILE CREEK

Fourmile Cutoff

Dry, sandy wash

Private Road. Turn out of wash.

07

375A

FOURMILE CREEK

03

376

376

376

376

6039

6039

6029

6029

Moderate

Difficult

Difficult

Lenhardy Cutoff

SEVENMILE CREEK

BLM LAND

1415 Difficult

375

375

375

02

Tunnels

6037

Moderate

TO HWY. 24

371

S

01

Start here

TO BUENA VISTA

371

TO CHUBB PARK

MCGEE GULCH

SHIELDS GULCH

Lenhardy Cutoff

376

305

315

376

376

08

09

24

307

Alt. Start

TO JOHNSON VILLAGE

Great camp spots with views

0 miles 1

BUENA VISTA

Start Here

01

371

371

TO HWY. 24

Arkansas River

N. Colorado Ave.

Main St.

24

Light

0 miles 0.5

129

Staging area. Get maps from dispenser.

Opening in fence to Chinaman Gulch.

Lots of banked curves—great fun!

View from top of optional Bald Mountain.

Short walk to cabin from Trail #1423

Ruby Mountain State Park Campground.

Washed out section of 185D.

Side trip to overlook off 185D.

Fourmile South 26

Getting There: From Denver, take Hwy. 285 towards Buena Vista. As you drop downhill from Trout Creek Pass, turn left on F.S. 307 after mile marker 222 before bridge. Go south 1.3 miles and turn left on 187. Continue 1.1 miles to staging area on right. If heading north on 285 from Johnson Village, turn right on 307 after mile marker 219. Go 1.5 miles and turn right on 187. To reach alternate start, exit Hwy. 285 north of Nathrop at F.S. 301. Go north 0.6 miles and turn right on 300. Go east, then south about 2.5 miles to Ruby Mountain State Park. Parking lot is just beyond park. ATVs cannot be ridden in park.

Staging/Camping: Unload at staging area at Fourmile sign. Check dispenser on sign for maps. To camp, continue on F.S. 300 about a mile to dispersed camp spots along road.

Difficulty: Trails 1423 and 1424 are a mix of easy and moderate terrain. Road 185D and Trail 1434 are usually moderate; however, after heavy rains, steep sections wash out and become difficult. Those looking for extreme challenge can try optional Chinaman Gulch. This popular 4-mile loop Jeep trail can be done on an ATV, but it is dangerous and winching is necessary. Optional Bald Mountain is very rough, but not too difficult.

Highlights: Great riding because key trails are for ATVs only, not Jeeps. (A few single-track routes, too.) Narrow, twisting trails with banked curves are fun to ride. Minimal whoops. Challenging, but not overly difficult. Great views from high points along route.

Time & Distance: As described, trail is 33.7 miles. Allow 4 to 6 hours.

Trail Description: Two great ATV loops connected by twisting and undulating forest roads. After riding two loops, continue on easy road to beautiful state park along the Arkansas River. On way back, take steep, rocky side trip up 9,700-ft. Bald Mountain.

Other nearby routes: Fourmile North, Trail #25, is just north of Hwy. 24/285. Four great mountain trails in Collegiate Peaks across valley.

Services: Closest gas and food at Johnson Village. Full services in Buena Vista. Toilets at Ruby Mountain State Park. Nothing on trail.

Directions: *(Shadowed portion of trail is described here.)*

WP	Mile	Action
01	**0.0**	*N38° 49.89 W105° 59.28´* Head south on F.S. 300.
	0.9	Stay right on main trail. Camp spots on left.
	1.4	Stay left. (Right ends at camp spot with view.)
02	**1.8**	*N38° 48.96 W106° 00.40´* Turn right on #1423.
	2.3	Stay right. (Trail #1424 goes left.)
	3.2	Short walk to cabin on left through opening in fence.
03	**5.5/0.0**	*N38° 48.12 W106° 03.02´* Stay left. (Optional side trip goes right to Chinaman Gulch, an extreme 4-mile loop for expert riders only. Winch required.)
	1.0	After downhill sandy wash, turn left on 300A.
	2.0	Turn left on ATV route #1424.
	3.7	Turn right on #1423
02	**4.2**	Back to Waypoint 02. Turn right on 300.
04	**5.4**	*N38° 48.04 W106° 00.88´* Turn left on 300.
05	**7.3/0.0**	*N38° 46.82´ W106° 01.29´* Hard left on 185D.
	1.9	After rough climb, take side trip right to overlook, then return and continue on 185D.
06	**3.6**	*N38° 45.84´ W105° 59.08´* Turn right on #1434.
	6.1	Stay left. (Road to right goes to high point.)
	7.7	Stay left where two steep, washed-out trails join.
	8.5	Stay right on 1434. (Option: Trail #1434A goes left on different route to Ruby Mountain State Park.)
07	**9.5/0.0**	*N38° 46.03´ W106° 02.36´* Turn left on F.S. 300 to Ruby Mountain State Park.
	0.4	Stay left. (Road to right is private.)
	1.4	Continue straight. (Trail #1434A on left.)
08	**2.3/0.0**	*N38° 45.13´ W106° 03.93´* Turn around at parking lot. No unlicensed vehicles in park. Walk to toilets.
09	**3.5**	*N38° 46.42´ W106° 01.90´* Continue straight on 300. (Optional 300B goes left to circle Bald Mountain. Adds about 4 miles to trip.)
05	**4.2**	Stay left on 300 where 185D goes right.
04	**6.1**	Turn right on 300 where 300A goes left.
01	**9.1**	Follow F.S. 300 on previous route back to start.

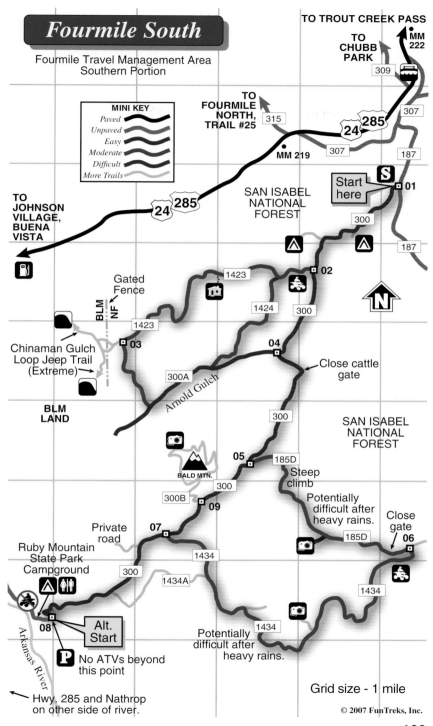

Fourmile South

Fourmile Travel Management Area
Southern Portion

MINI KEY
Paved
Unpaved
Easy
Moderate
Difficult
More Trails

TO TROUT CREEK PASS

TO CHUBB PARK

MM 222

309

307

24 **285**

307

187

Start here — S — 01

187

300

TO FOURMILE NORTH, TRAIL #25

315

MM 219

SAN ISABEL NATIONAL FOREST

24 **285**

TO JOHNSON VILLAGE, BUENA VISTA

02

1423

1424

300

300

Gated Fence

BLM NF

1423

03

Chinaman Gulch Loop Jeep Trail (Extreme)

BLM LAND

300A

Arnold Gulch

04

Close cattle gate

300

SAN ISABEL NATIONAL FOREST

BALD MTN.

05

185D

Steep climb

300

300B

09

Potentially difficult after heavy rains.

Close gate

06

185D

Private road

07

Ruby Mountain State Park Campground

300

1434

1434A

1434

08

Alt. Start

P No ATVs beyond this point

Arkansas River

Potentially difficult after heavy rains.

1434

Grid size - 1 mile

Hwy. 285 and Nathrop on other side of river.

© 2007 FunTreks, Inc.

N

133

Taylor Park—the wild west at its best.

Taylor Park Trading Post.

Easier section of Timberline Trail.

Crossing Red Mountain Creek.

Backway to Tincup.

Lower end Slaughterhouse Gulch.

Frenchy's Cafe. Popular stop in Tincup.

Difficult Sanford-Timberline Trail.

Getting There: From traffic light on Highway 24 and Main Street in Buena Vista, head west on Cottonwood Pass Road, C.R. 306. Pavement ends at the pass. Continue about 13 miles down other side on dirt road and turn left on paved Taylor River Road 742. Go south another 2 miles and turn left on 765 towards Trading Post. Park in the semi-circular grassy area outside the split-rail fence.

Consider two alternate staging areas. As you start down from Cottonwood Pass on 209, go 8.6 miles and turn left at sign for Stage Stop Meadows. Go through trees to clearing. A maze of roads goes down the mountain. Second alternate staging is at parking lot at end of 209.

Staging/Camping: No camping at main staging area. An RV park with full hook-ups is located past the trading post, up the hill on the right. Cabins are also available to rent. Two Forest Service campgrounds are located north of the reservoir on Taylor River Road. You'll also find great dispersed camp spots along this road. An unimproved F.S. camping area is located on right 2.3 miles east on 765.

Difficulty: Much of the route is easy; however, Timberline Trail and Slaughterhouse Gulch have sections that are narrow, steep and rocky. Optional Sanford-Timberline Trail is extremely difficult for ATVs.

Highlights: Broad valley surrounded by rugged mountains. Incredibly varied terrain. Visit historic town of Tincup. Carry extra gas.

Time & Distance: Route described here is 45.3 miles and takes 4-5 hours.

Route Description: Take a quick loop tour of northern Taylor Park then explore a complex network of roads on the hills east of the reservoir. Conclude with final loop through Union Park to Tincup and back.

Other nearby routes: Tincup/Hancock Loop, Trail #28, crosses this trail in Tincup. Hundreds of miles of other roads and trails in the area. You can ride to Aspen via F.S. Roads 742, 761 and 123. Incredible Italian Creek Road 759 goes almost to Crested Butte. Recommended map: *Latitude 40° Crested Butte/Taylor Park Recreation Topo Map.*

Services: Gas and supplies at Taylor Park Trading Post. Supplies but no gas at Tincup General Store. Restaurants at both locations.

Directions: *(Shadowed portion of trail is described here.)*

WP	Mile	Action
01	0.0	*N38° 49.21 W106° 33.49´* From Trading Post, head north and bear right uphill towards RV park.
	0.3	At RV park, turn left on gravel road.
	0.8	Go downhill, turn right through gate on OHV trail.
	1.7	Bear right following 2-track road along paved 742.
	2.0	Cross paved 742 to parking lot at end of Cottonwood Pass Road 209. From this point, ride north on gravel road 742.
02	6.4/0.0	*N38° 53.68 W106° 34.21´* Turn right on 742.8F.
	3.8	Arrive at Pieplant Townsite. Follow ATV trail around cabins to left. (No ATVs allowed to right.)
	5.2	After rocky downhill, trail goes left past hiking trail.
	7.3	Bear right, then cross Red Mountain Creek.
	7.5	Stay right past camp spots to Red Mountain Rd. 742.8H. Turn right and follow better road downhhill.
	8.7	Turn left on Taylor River Road 742. Ride south.
03	14.4/0.0	*N38° 51.16´ W106° 33.90´* Turn left on Texas Creek Road 755. Ignore roads that branch right.
04	1.5	*N38° 51.30´ W106° 32.72´* Main road swings left and drops downhill to clearing. Turn right here and cross wide creek. Head south on rougher road.
	1.7	Stay left. (Difficult road goes right.)
	2.0	Turn right on 755.1A.
	2.6	Continue straight across Cottonwood Pass Road 209.
	3.9	Stay right as you join better road 209.1G
	4.5	Stay right on better road.
	5.0	Stay right downhill on 587.1 past residential area.
	5.8	Bear left on major road 765. Head south.
05	6.0/0.0	*N38° 48.89 W106° 31.77´* After small wooden bridge, continue south off 765 onto C.R. 55. Follow signs to Union Park.
06	1.3	*N38° 48.91´ W106° 33.09´* Hard left uphill on 752.
	2.6	After cattle guard, take center road at 3-way fork.
07	4.2/0.0	*N38° 46.99´ W106° 33.87´* Turn left on lesser 764 towards Slaughterhouse Gulch.
	0.1	Bear right and cross creek. Begin climb up rougher road.
	3.4	Pass through gate. Close it. Road gets wider and levels out.
08	6.0/0.0	*N38° 44.80´ W106° 29.11´* Turn left on Cumberland Pass Road 765 towards Tincup.
	0.8	Continue north through Tincup at church. F.S. 267 goes east.
	4.2	Continue straight. (Right on 725 goes to difficult Sanford Trail.
01	8.3	Follow 765 back to start.

136

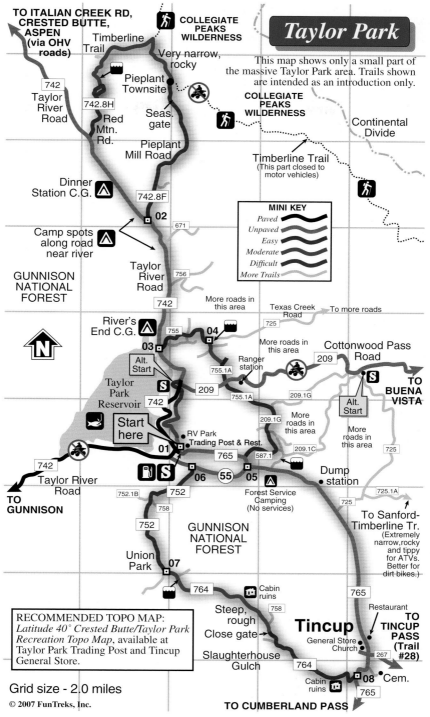

TO ITALIAN CREEK RD,
CRESTED BUTTE,
ASPEN
(via OHV
roads)

Timberline
Trail

COLLEGIATE
PEAKS
WILDERNESS

Taylor Park

Very narrow,
rocky

This map shows only a small part of
the massive Taylor Park area. Trails shown
are intended as an introduction only.

742
Taylor
River
Road

Pieplant
Townsite

742.8H

COLLEGIATE
PEAKS
WILDERNESS

Red
Mtn.
Rd.

Seas.
gate

Continental
Divide

Pieplant
Mill Road

Timberline Trail
(This part closed to
motor vehicles)

Dinner
Station C.G.

742.8F

02

671

MINI KEY
Paved
Unpaved
Easy
Moderate
Difficult
More Trails

Camp spots
along road
near river

Taylor
River
Road

756

GUNNISON
NATIONAL
FOREST

742

More roads in
this area

Texas Creek
Road

To more roads

River's
End C.G.

755

04

725

N

03

More roads in
this area

Cottonwood Pass
Road

Alt.
Start

755.1A

Ranger
station

209

S

TO
BUENA
VISTA

Taylor
Park
Reservoir

S

209

755.1A

209.1G

Alt.
Start

742

Start
here

209.1G

More
roads in
this area

More
roads in
this area

725

01

RV Park
Trading Post & Rest.

765

587.1

209.1C

Dump
station

742

S

06

55

05

725.1A

TO
GUNNISON

Taylor River
Road

752.1B

752

Forest Service
Camping
(No services)

725

758

To Sanford-
Timberline Tr.
(Extremely
narrow, rocky
and tippy
for ATVs.
Better for
dirt bikes.)

GUNNISON
NATIONAL
FOREST

Union
Park

07

764

758

Cabin
ruins

765

Restaurant
TO
TINCUP
PASS
(Trail
#28)

RECOMMENDED TOPO MAP:
*Latitude 40° Crested Butte/Taylor Park
Recreation Topo Map*, available at
Taylor Park Trading Post and Tincup
General Store.

Steep,
rough

Close gate

Slaughterhouse
Gulch

Tincup

General Store
Church

764

267

Cem.

08

Grid size - 2.0 miles

© 2007 FunTreks, Inc.

Cabin
ruins

TO CUMBERLAND PASS

765

137

Staging area fills quickly in the summer.

Riders go past St. Elmo General Store.

Crossing Tincup Pass.

Mirror Lake looking south to Tincup Pass.

General Store in Tincup.

Cumberland Pass Road 765.

Mine on side road near Cumberland Pass.

Hancock Pass route is steep and rocky.

138

Tincup/Hancock Loop 28

Getting There: Just south of Nathrop, turn west from Hwy. 285 onto County Road 162. Go 15.4 miles to staging area with toilet on left. (Nathrop is 8 miles south of Buena Vista.)

Staging/Camping: This area is very busy on summer weekends. Finding a place to park and camp can be a challenge. Don't park along 162 before the staging area; ATVs are not allowed on this portion of road. Don't park in St. Elmo or on private land just east of town. Your best bet is to park at wide spots along 295. Make advance reservations for Forest Service campgrounds. Dispersed camping is allowed along 267, but your tow vehicle will need high clearance. You can also camp along 295 beyond a sign about 1.5 miles south of staging area.

Difficulty: Much of the route is easy, but the climbs over Tincup and Hancock Passes are moderately rocky and steep. These 12,000-ft. passes can be blocked by snow into July. Many difficult trails branch off from the primary route described here. See map.

Highlights: Unforgettable high-country tour of once bustling mining area. F.S. 839 follows old railroad route to Alpine Tunnel. See restored water tower and many other mine structures. Visit historic mining towns of St. Elmo, Tincup and Pitkin. Carry extra gas.

Time & Distance: Loop measures 51.3 miles and takes about 6 hours. Add plenty of extra time for sightseeing and side trails.

Trail Description: Begin with trip over Tincup Pass into Tincup. Head south over Cumberland Pass, then east on long climb to Alpine Tunnel. Finally, climb over Hancock Pass and return to start.

Other nearby routes: This route connects to Taylor Park, Trail #27, and Pomeroy Lakes, Trail #29. Mt. Antero, Trail #30, is just east on 162. Many side trails to explore including Napolean Pass, 765.2B, to Cumberland Pass, Tomichi Pass, Iron Chest Mine and Grizzly Lake. Sanford-Timberline Trail is extremely difficult for ATVs.

Services: Full services in Buena Vista. Gas and supplies at the Mt. Princeton Hot Springs Country Store on 162 and in Pitkin. General store and ATV rental in St. Elmo. Tincup has a general store but no gas.

139

Directions: *(Shadowed portion of trail is described here.)*

WP	Mile	Action
01	**0.0**	*N38° 42.32 W106° 20.35´* Head west from staging area and stay right downhill into St. Elmo.
	0.4	In center of St. Elmo, turn right and cross wooden bridge, then turn left.
	0.6	Follow signs on rocky road uphill to Tincup Pass.
02	**6.8**	*N38° 42.56 W106° 26.07´* Continue north over Tincup Pass.
	7.5	Road bends to left. (Right goes down difficult Old Tincup route.)
	8.4	Stay left. (Old Tincup route rejoins on right.)
	9.8	Stay right across creek. Stay on east side of lake.
	10.3	Continue straight past parking lot and campground.
	10.7	Continue straight. Toilet on right. (Sanford-Timberline Trail departs left of toilet.
03	**13.6/0.0**	*N38° 45.28´ W106° 28.82´* Turn left in center of Tincup at white church with steeple.
	0.2	Continue straight. (Option: Lesser road to left goes to Tincup Cemetery and Napoleon Pass.)
	0.3	Stay right on 765. (Option: Lesser road to left is interesting back way to Cumberland Pass.)
04	**8.0**	*N38° 41.36´ W106° 29.05´* Cumberland Pass. Continue south. (See mine on side road to left.)
05	**16.1/0.0**	*N38° 37.50´ W106° 28.56´* Turn left on 839 to Alpine Tunnel. (Straight goes to Pitkin in 3 miles.)
06	**7.7/0.0**	*N38° 36.82´ W106° 23.41´* Stay left on 839 to see Alpine Tunnel in 2.3 miles. Then return and head uphill on 888 towards Hancock Pass.
	0.7	Bear left on 266 for Hancock Pass. (Option: Right goes up narrow Tomichi Pass and beyond.)
07	**1.7**	*N38° 36.80´ W106° 23.96´* After steep, rocky climb, arrive at Hancock Pass. Continue north.
08	**3.9**	*N38° 38.30´ W106° 21.68´* Turn left at T to Hancock Townsite, then continue north on 295. (Option: Right on 295 goes to Hancock Lake.)
	9.5	Bear right on 162 after passing entrance points to optional Iron Chest and Grizzly Jeep Trails.
01	**9.6**	Return to staging area.

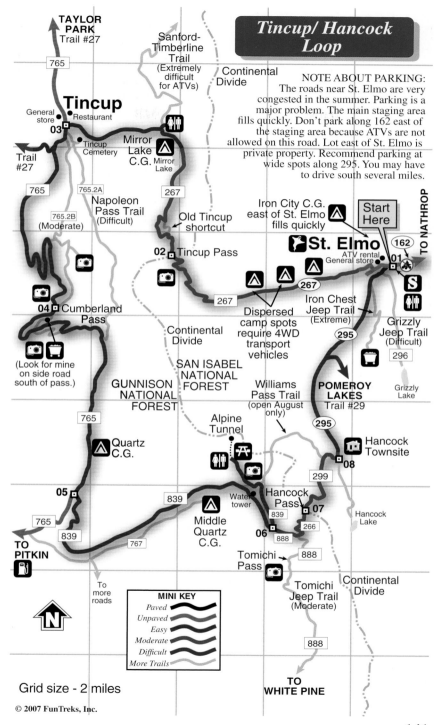

Tincup/ Hancock Loop

TAYLOR PARK Trail #27

765

Sanford-Timberline Trail (Extremely difficult for ATVs)

Continental Divide

NOTE ABOUT PARKING: The roads near St. Elmo are very congested in the summer. Parking is a major problem. The main staging area fills quickly. Don't park along 162 east of the staging area because ATVs are not allowed on this road. Lot east of St. Elmo is private property. Recommend parking at wide spots along 295. You may have to drive south several miles.

Tincup

General store   Restaurant
03
Tincup Cemetery

Mirror Lake C.G.   Mirror Lake

Trail #27

765   765.2A

765.2B (Moderate)

Napoleon Pass Trail (Difficult)

267

Old Tincup shortcut

02 Tincup Pass

267

267

Iron City C.G. east of St. Elmo fills quickly

Start Here

St. Elmo
ATV rental
General store   **01**

S

TO NATHROP

162

Dispersed camp spots require 4WD transport vehicles

Iron Chest Jeep Trail (Extreme)

295

Grizzly Jeep Trail (Difficult)

296

04 Cumberland Pass

(Look for mine on side road south of pass.)

Continental Divide

SAN ISABEL NATIONAL FOREST

GUNNISON NATIONAL FOREST

765

Quartz C.G.

Williams Pass Trail (open August only)

POMEROY LAKES
Trail #29

295

Grizzly Lake

Hancock Townsite
08

Alpine Tunnel

299

05

765

839

839

767

Middle Quartz C.G.

Water tower

Hancock Pass

839

06   888

07

266

Hancock Lake

TO PITKIN

To more roads

Tomichi Pass

888

Tomichi Jeep Trail (Moderate)

Continental Divide

888

TO WHITE PINE

MINI KEY
Paved
Unpaved
Easy
Moderate
Difficult
More Trails

N

Grid size - 2 miles

© 2007 FunTreks, Inc.

141

Abandoned cabin above Romley.

Mary Murphy Mill. Look but don't touch.

Pomeroy Lakes are above timberline.

Group returns from fishing and camping.

Mary Murphy Mine near 12,000 ft.

Bunkhouse at millsite.

Narrow road that climbs to mine.

St. Elmo is a popular summer destination. Finding a place to park can be a challenge.

Pomeroy Lakes

29

Getting There: Just south of Nathrop, turn west from Hwy. 285 onto County Road 162. Go 15.4 miles to staging area with toilet on left. Continue southwest, bearing left on C.R. 295. Go about 3 miles and turn left uphill on rough road, following sign to Mary Murphy Mine.

Staging/Camping: Unload at staging area. If full, look for wide spot along 295. No unlicensed vehicles are allowed on 162 east of staging area. Camping is allowed along 295 after sign about 1.5 miles after staging area. Reservations recommended for nearby F.S. campgrounds. To avoid crowds, consider accessing from Taylor Park side, Trail #27.

Difficulty: Lower portion of trail is easy to moderate. As you climb, the trail gets steeper and rougher. The road to Pomeroy Lakes is very rocky with one steep obstacle. Reaching Mary Murphy Mine requires climbing a steep, narrow shelf road.

Highlights: Photogenic mine buildings remain in relatively good condition. Short, but difficult climb to large lakes above timberline. Great views from Mary Murphy Mine near 12,000 ft. A short but fun ride.

Time & Distance: Round trip is only 6.3 miles. Allow about 2 hours.

Trail Description: Most people visit the primary mine buildings within the first mile, but few continue uphill to the mine. The narrow shelf road going to the mine is very narrow for Jeeps, but perfect for ATVs. The trip to the lakes is for experienced riders only.

Other nearby routes: This trip can be combined with Tincup/Hancock Loop, Trail #28, or Mt. Antero, Baldwin Lakes, Trail #30. Just over the ridge above Mary Murphy Mine is Iron Chest Mine, reached via the well-known and extremely difficult Iron Chest Jeep Trail.

Services: Full services in Buena Vista and Salida. Gas and supplies at the Mt. Princeton Hot Springs Country Store on 162. General store and ATV rental in St. Elmo. Carry extra gas.

Historical Highlights: Mary Murphy Mine was a top producing mine that supported the town of Romley. The area flourished between 1870 and the early 1900s. The main part of Romley was located in a meadow below C.R. 295. Romley was also known as "Red Town," because all buildings in town were painted red with white trim. The railroad removed its tracks in 1926, but it was not until 1982 that the town was torn down by its owners.

Directions: *(Shadowed portion of trail is described here.)*

WP	Mile	Action
01	**0.0**	*N38° 40.39 W106° 22.00´* From Hancock Road 295, turn hard left uphill following sign to Mary Murphy Mine.
	0.2	Continue uphill on rocky road. The town of Romley was once located to the left.
02	**0.8**	*N38° 40.04´ W106° 21.47´* Continue straight. Pass between buildings that remain from Mary Murphy Mill. (Private property; do not enter or get close to buildings.)
	0.9	Bear right on 297.2, marked as dead-end road.
	1.2	Stay left. Private road to right.
03	**1.5**	*N38° 39.59´ W106° 21.13´* Stay right. You'll come back to this point soon.
	1.7	Continue straight past grave on right.
	1.8	Continue straight. Road goes left to camp spot.
04	**2.0**	*N38° 39.31´ W106° 20.72´* Turn left uphill on difficult rocky road. Right dead ends next to meadow.
	2.4	Stay left up toughest part of trail.
05	**2.8**	*N38° 38.91´ W106° 20.38´* Stop and turn around at circular area. No motor vehicles beyond this point. Hike to lakes.
03	**4.1/0.0**	Return to Waypoint 03. Turn right uphill. Road climbs steeply and is very narrrow.
06	**0.5**	*N38° 40.01´ W106° 21.09´* Stay right.
	0.6	Mary Murphy Mine. Stop where you can turn around safely.
03	**0.7**	Turn right to see remains of tram cable towers.
	0.9	Turn around at flat mining area. Return down the mountain the way you came.
01	**2.2**	Back to start. Turn right on 295 to return to staging area or to visit St. Elmo.

144

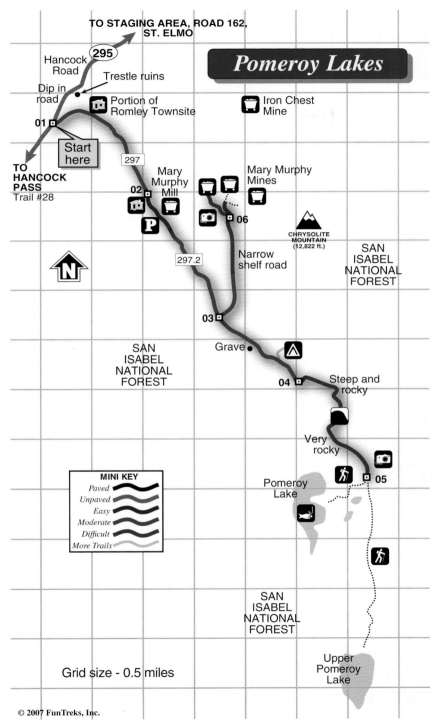

Pomeroy Lakes

TO STAGING AREA, ROAD 162, ST. ELMO

295 Hancock Road

Trestle ruins

Dip in road

Portion of Romley Townsite

Iron Chest Mine

01

Start here

297

TO HANCOCK PASS
Trail #28

Mary Murphy Mill

Mary Murphy Mines

02

P

06

CHRYSOLITE MOUNTAIN
(12,822 ft.)

SAN ISABEL NATIONAL FOREST

297.2

Narrow shelf road

03

SAN ISABEL NATIONAL FOREST

Grave

04

Steep and rocky

Very rocky

05

Pomeroy Lake

MINI KEY
Paved
Unpaved
Easy
Moderate
Difficult
More Trails

SAN ISABEL NATIONAL FOREST

Grid size - 0.5 miles

Upper Pomeroy Lake

N

© 2007 FunTreks, Inc.

Crossing Baldwin Creek towards Mt. Antero.

The first switchback.

A mountain of switchbacks.

Final climb to top.

Road ends at 13,800 ft.

Side trip to Browns Lake.

Looking down on Baldwin Lakes.

Mine above Baldwin Lakes.

Mt. Antero, Baldwin Lakes

30

Getting There: Just south of Nathrop, turn west from Hwy. 285 onto County Road 162. (Nathrop is 8 miles south of Buena Vista.) Watch for sign to Mt. Antero at 12.3 miles. Turn left up F.S. Road 277.

Staging/Camping: No parking area near trailhead. If you can find a wide spot on 162 close by, you can park on the side of the road and unload. If not, unload at the trailhead and park down the road. You are not allowed to ride your ATV along 162.

Difficulty: This trip is very rocky but there are no major obstacles. The switchbacks up Mt. Antero are steep, narrow and scary but fairly smooth until the last half mile. This last section is prone to washouts, so inspect the route ahead before going too far. The road to the mine above Baldwin Lakes is also very rocky but it is not extremely steep.

Highlights: You'll be telling your friends about this one—a true Colorado high. Go on a clear day to enjoy the fantastic views. Allow enough time for side trips to Mount White, Browns Lake and Boulder Mountain. Camp and fish at Browns Lake and along Baldwin Creek.

Time & Distance: Basic route is 23.2 miles and takes 4 to 5 hours. Round trips to Browns Lake and Boulder Mountain add 7 miles and 10 miles, respectively.

Trail Description: Trail starts at 9400 ft. and climbs to 13,800 ft. (See page 15 for carburetor adjustment information.) The first 4 miles are in the trees with little to see. Soon everything changes as you climb high above timberline. It is best to ride Mt. Antero in the morning. Afternoons in Colorado tend to be cloudy with thunderstorms. If you see lightning in the distance, descend the mountain immediately.

Other nearby routes: Continue west on 162 to staging area for Tincup/Hancock Loop, Trail #28, and Pomeroy Lakes, Trail #29. East of Buena Vista, don't miss the Fourmile area, Trails #25 and #26. West of Buena Vista is massive Taylor Park, Trail #27.

Services: Full services in Buena Vista and Salida. Gas and supplies at the Mt. Princeton Hot Springs Country Store on 162. General store and ATV rental in St. Elmo. Carry extra gas.

Directions: *(Shadowed portion of trail is described here.)*

WP	Mile	Action
01	**0.0**	*N38° 42.60 W106° 17.50´* From C.R. 162, turn left at sign for Mt. Antero and follow rocky F.S. 277 uphill.
02	**1.2**	*N38° 42.22´ W106° 16.52´* Continue straight. (Optional Boulder Mountain Road goes right.)
03	**2.8**	*N38° 40.95´ W106° 16.37´* Turn left and cross creek to climb Mt. Antero. (Straight goes to Baldwin Lakes.)
	4.3	Come out of trees and start up first switch-back. Proceed with caution.
04	**6.3**	*N38° 39.71´ W106° 15.47´* Turn left uphill on 278A. (Option: Straight goes downhill to Browns Lake in 3.5 miles.)
	6.4	Stay left on 278A. (F.S. 278B goes right to Mount White.
	6.8	Stay left uphill. Trail gets steeper and rougher. Check conditions before proceeding. Erosion can make this section difficult or even impassable. Timid riders may want to stop here.
05	**7.6**	*N38° 40.07´ W106° 14.93´* Arrive at top via choice of several different forks. Stop here. Elevation at this point is 13,800 ft. Just north is the actual top of Mt. Antero at 14,289 ft.
03	**17.2/0.0**	Return to Waypoint 03 at creek crossing. Turn left to Baldwin Lakes.
	0.9	Start across rocky talus slopes.
	1.5	Stay left. Dead end road goes right to mine.
	2.2	Bear right at parking lot for hiking trail. Road gets very rocky and may be blocked by snow.
06	**3.3**	*N38° 39.92´ W106° 18.71´* Road ends at small mine building.
01	**6.0**	Return to start.

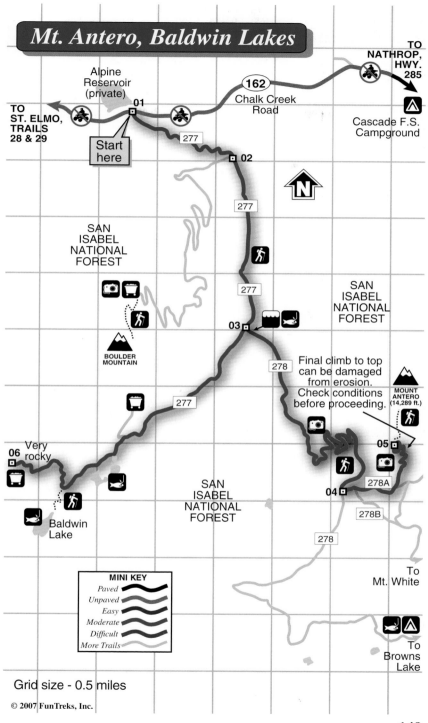

Mt. Antero, Baldwin Lakes

TO
NATHROP,
HWY.
285

Alpine
Reservoir
(private)

162
Chalk Creek
Road

01

TO
ST. ELMO,
TRAILS
28 & 29

Cascade F.S.
Campground

**Start
here**

277

02

277

N

SAN
ISABEL
NATIONAL
FOREST

277

SAN
ISABEL
NATIONAL
FOREST

03

278

Final climb to top
can be damaged
from erosion.
Check conditions
before proceeding.

MOUNT
ANTERO
(14,289 ft.)

277

BOULDER
MOUNTAIN

05

Very
rocky

06

278A

04

278B

Baldwin
Lake

SAN
ISABEL
NATIONAL
FOREST

278

To
Mt. White

MINI KEY
Paved
Unpaved
Easy
Moderate
Difficult
More Trails

To
Browns
Lake

Grid size - 0.5 miles

© 2007 FunTreks, Inc.

149

Staging area.

First part of route is an easy cruise.

Nearing top of Toll Road.

Restored cabin at Exchequer Townsite.

Picnic area north of Bonanza.

Upper section of Rawley Mine (Wpt. 08).

Unidentified mine on side road.

Side roads above timberline at Whale Hill.

Open stretch of alternate return route.

Otto Mears Toll Road ㉛

Getting There: From Poncha Springs west of Salida, head south on Highway 285 about 5 miles. Turn right on County Road 200 and go southwest until the road forks at 2.2 miles. Bear left around the corner to a large staging area with toilet.

Staging/Camping: Unload at staging area. No camping here. Excellent dispersed camping spots along 201 and west on 203.

Difficulty: The main route described here is easy the entire way with occasional minor rocky stretches. Side roads south of the Rawley Mines are difficult, narrow, tippy and steep. The alternate return route on 876 is mostly easy; however, a few places are rocky and steep. This route is not described in detail. Follow map.

Highlights: Dense mining area with many standing structures of historical significance. To learn more, read information boards at Shirley Townsite and Bonanza. Route follows 1890s toll road built by Otto Mears. Road climbs over scenic ridge above 11,000 feet.

Time & Distance: Round trip covers 32 miles and takes 3 to 4 hours. Add extra time for side roads and alternate return route.

Trail Description: Follow graded F.S. 201 south. Road gets rougher after 3 miles. At 5.5 miles, turn sharply left and begin climb up Toll Road Gulch. Enter Rio Grande N. F. and begin descent to Bonanza. Return from Bonanza and climb easy roads to Rawley Mines. Many more mines on side roads. Climb to Whale Hill over 12,000 ft.

Other nearby routes: Explore F.S. 203 southwest of the staging area (not described in this book). This easy 7.5-mile road climbs the back way to Marshall Pass along scenic Poncha Creek. Great camping and fishing along this road.

Services: Gas up in Salida or Poncha Springs. Modern vault toilets at staging area and at picnic area north of Bonanza.

Historical Highlights: Bonanza was a town of 500 people in the early 1880s with over a hundred buildings, including 6 saloons, a drugstore, post office, hardware store, school, town hall, furniture store and 2 hotels. As the silver mines faded, the population dropped to below 100. A second boom occurred in the 1920s with the discovery of new ore at the Rawley Mine. At that time a cable tram was built to carry ore to a mill in Shirley. Bonanza faded away in the 1930s and was destroyed by fire in 1937.

151

Directions: *(Shadowed portion of trail is described here.)*

WP	Mile	Action
01	**0.0**	*N38° 25.19 W106° 07.76´* Head south from staging area along wide, graded F.S. 201.
	3.0	Road gets rougher. Stay right.
	5.2	Pass through wooded area with great camp spots.
02	**5.5**	*N38° 21.81 W106° 10.62´* Hard left uphill at sign for "Toll Road Gulch."
	9.3	Cross talus slope at first break in trees. Views to north include Mount Ouray, near 14,000 ft.
	9.7	At highest point of trail. Enter Rio Grande N.F. Sign says Squirrel Creek Road 869.
	11.2	Stay right downhill.
03	**12.3**	*N38° 19.72 W106° 08.74´* Continue straight on 869, now a better road. (Road 876 that joins on left is alternate return route.)
	13.2	Stay right.
	13.4	Modern picnic area with toilet on right.
	14.1	Continue straight. F.S. 862 joins on right.
04	**14.2**	*N38° 18.40 W106° 08.83´* Continue straight. (Restored cabin of Exchequer Townsite on left. Gated road right of cabin goes to interesting cemetery.)
05	**15.2**	*N38° 17.66 W106° 08.55´* Inhabited town of Bonanza. Read information board that explains history of area, then turn around.
04	**16.2/0.0**	Return to Waypoint 04 and turn right uphill.
	0.9	Hard left up switchback. (Narrow road straight ahead is difficult but fun route to Superior and Whale Mines where buildings remain.)
06	**1.2**	*N38° 18.68 W106° 08.45´* Stay right uphill.
07	**2.5**	*N38° 19.30 W106° 07.54´* Bear left uphill; follow sign to Round Mountain. (First explore Rawley Mine complex on right below—great photogenic buildings. Just around corner to right, marked "Spring Creek," is difficult alternate way to Whale and Superior Mines.)
	3.4	Turn right.
08	**3.5/0.0**	*N38° 19.55 W106°07.50´* More buildings of Rawley Mine—looks like ghost town. Turn around and return to Waypoint 06. (Or, explore many more roads in area.)
06	**2.3**	Turn hard right on shortcut back to 869.
	2.7	Stay right and continue north on 869. Return the way you came or via longer, more complex alternate route 876.
01	**15.9**	Return to start. (Alternate route is 2 miles longer.)

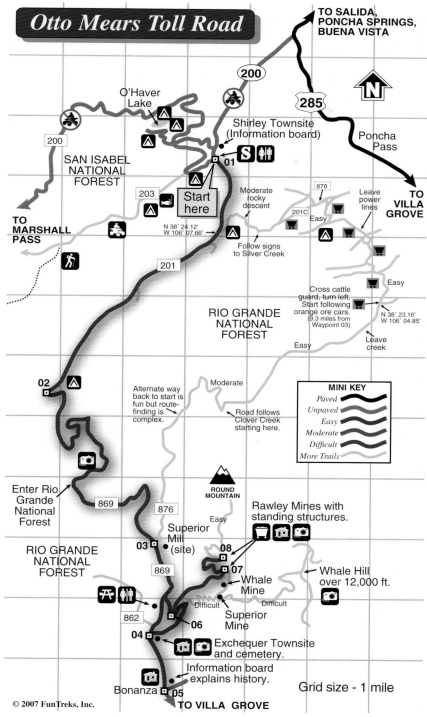

Otto Mears Toll Road

TO SALIDA,
PONCHA SPRINGS,
BUENA VISTA

200

285

N

O'Haver Lake

Shirley Townsite
(Information board)

Poncha Pass

S

01

200

SAN ISABEL
NATIONAL
FOREST

203

Start here

Moderate rocky descent

878

Leave power lines

TO VILLA GROVE

201C

Easy

TO MARSHALL PASS

N 38' 24.12'
W 106' 07.66'

201

Follow signs to Silver Creek

Cross cattle guard, turn left. Start following orange ore cars. (9.3 miles from Waypoint 03)

Easy

RIO GRANDE
NATIONAL
FOREST

N 38' 23.16'
W 106' 04.85'

Leave creek

Easy

02

Alternate way back to start is fun but route-finding is complex.

Moderate

Road follows Clover Creek starting here.

MINI KEY
Paved
Unpaved
Easy
Moderate
Difficult
More Trails

Enter Rio Grande National Forest

869

876

ROUND MOUNTAIN

Rawley Mines with standing structures.

RIO GRANDE
NATIONAL
FOREST

03

Superior Mill (site)

869

08

Easy

07

Whale Hill over 12,000 ft.

Whale Mine

862

06

Difficult

Superior Mine

Difficult

04

Exchequer Townsite and cemetery.

Bonanza

05

Information board explains history.

Grid size - 1 mile

TO VILLA GROVE

© 2007 FunTreks, Inc.

153

Turn off Highway 50 at this store.

Views heading west on Trail #6026.

Narrow winding trails are great fun.

Raised cattle guards instead of gates.

Climbing steep switchbacks on Trail #6036.

Trail #6040 levels out as you near the top.

Safety strap used at this steep spot.

154

Texas Creek

Getting There: Take Highway 50 about 23 miles west of Canon City (about 60 miles west of Pueblo). Turn right on County Road 27 next to store at Texas Creek across from intersection of Highway 69. After bridge, swing right, then left over railroad tracks. Staging area is on right about a half mile from Highway 50.

Staging/Camping: Staging area is large with plenty of room to park. BLM dispersed camping rules apply in the area.

Difficulty: Primary roads are rocky in places but generally easy. ATV routes vary from easy to very difficult. Novice riders should not attempt sections shown in red. Even skilled riders may have trouble with the steepest sections. Don't ride alone.

Highlights: Many of the trails in the area have been designed specifically for ATVs and dirt bikes. Narrow trails and steep terrain provide an exceptional riding experience. Although not large, the area delivers a great deal of fun per mile.

Time & Distance: Complete trip is 26.3 miles. Allow about 4 hours.

Trail Description: You'll head west along a rough but scenic ridge that looks down on the Arkansas River Valley. Follow a sandy wash north, then climb steeply on a loop route that features a brutal descent down a short, rocky staircase. Negotiate steep, tight switchbacks on your way to a second northern loop that climbs above 8700 ft. Novice riders will find the easy routes fun and stimulating with small challenges, high climbs and great scenery.

Other nearby routes: Otto Mears Toll Road, Trail # 31, is just 42 miles west. Buena Vista, with six outstanding trails covered in this book, is only 53 miles away. Highway 50 runs along the Arkansas River, a popular recreation area best known for rafting.

Services: Full services in Canon City and Salida. General store and small restaurant at Texas Creek. The store had gas pumps, but they were not functioning during the author's visit. Gas is usually available at Cotopaxi, seven miles west on Highway 50. Plans call for a restroom to be built at the staging area.

Directions: *(Shadowed portion of trail is described here.)*

WP	Mile	Action
01	**0.0**	*N38° 24.93 W105° 35.18´* Head north through staging area and join wider CR 27. Continue north.
02	**0.2**	*N38° 25.03 W105° 35.34´* Turn left up steep, short hill.
	0.3	At top of hill, turn left on 6021.
	0.4	Turn right on 6026.
	1.5	Continue straight where 6022 goes left downhill.
	2.1	Turn right on better road
03	**2.4**	*N38° 25.01 W105° 36.76´* Turn right off main road onto steep, rocky Tucker Trail 6035. (To bypass, continue to sandy wash.)
	2.8	Turn right in Reese Gulch and follow dry, sandy wash north.
	3.3	Stay right. Left is closed.
05	**3.6**	Continue straight where 6036 goes right. You'll come back to this point soon.
	3.8	Driver's choice. Stay right.
04	**4.2**	*N38° 26.32 W105° 37.23´* Stay right at start of loop.
	5.1	Trail begins steep climb out of wash.
	6.9	Descend steep, rocky ledges. Have assistant use safety strap to stop ATV from flipping forward. Stack rocks to fill gaps.
	8.7	Loop complete. Stay right in wash.
05	**9.1**	*N38° 25.86 W105° 37.15´* Turn left up very steep 6036.
	10.2	Reach top of steep ridge and start back down.
	11.2	End of 6036. Turn right to reach C.R. 27. (Left also goes to 27.)
	11.3	Turn left on C.R. 27.
	11.6	Bear right twice and stay on C.R. 27. Left is 6040.
06	**12.0**	*N38° 26.56 W105° 36.07´* Bear right on C.R. 27.
07	**14.7/0.0**	*N38° 27.95 W105° 35.13´* Turn left up Bull Gulch on 6061.
	0.8	Good size rocky ledge to climb.
	1.0	Stay right up steep 6061 where dirt bike trail 6062 goes left.
	2.3	After climbing to top of ridge, descend and connect with 6040.
08	**3.9**	*N38° 29.19 W105° 36.89´* Turn left on Trail 6057.
	4.1	Stay right on 6057 where 6057A goes left. Descend steeply.
	4.5	Turn left at triangular intersection.
	4.7	Continue downhill where 6057A rejoins on left.
09	**4.8**	*N38° 28.63 W105° 36.93´* Stay right on 6056. (6062 on left.)
	6.1	Bear left. You are now on 6040. Continue downhill.
	6.4	Stay right where 6055 goes left.
	8.9	Stay right on 6040. (Left is alternate way to same place.)
01	**11.6**	Continue downhill on C.R. 27 to staging area.

156

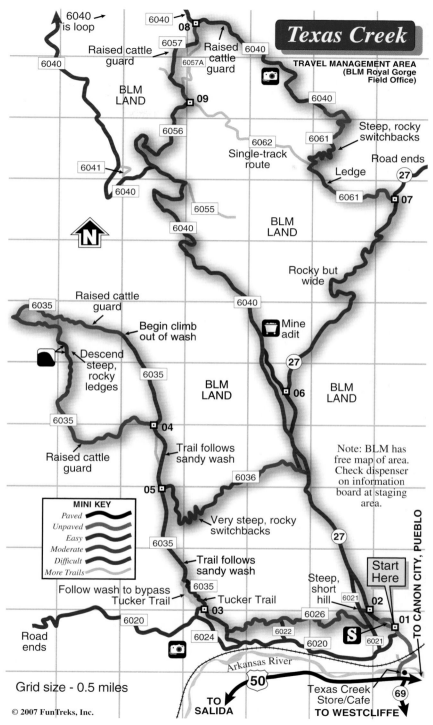

Texas Creek

TRAVEL MANAGEMENT AREA
(BLM Royal Gorge Field Office)

6040 is loop

6040

08

6040

6057

Raised cattle guard

Raised cattle guard

6057A

6040

6040

BLM LAND

09

6056

6040

Steep, rocky switchbacks

6062

6061

Single-track route

Road ends

27

6041

Ledge

6040

6061

07

6055

N

6040

BLM LAND

Rocky but wide

Raised cattle guard

6035

6040

Begin climb out of wash

Mine adit

Descend steep, rocky ledges

6035

27

BLM LAND

BLM LAND

6035

06

04

Raised cattle guard

Trail follows sandy wash

Note: BLM has free map of area. Check dispenser on information board at staging area.

6036

05

MINI KEY
Paved
Unpaved
Easy
Moderate
Difficult
More Trails

Very steep, rocky switchbacks

27

6035

Trail follows sandy wash

Start Here

Follow wash to bypass Tucker Trail

6035

Steep, short hill

6021

02

Tucker Trail

Tucker Trail

6026

01

6020

03

S

6024

6022

6021

Road ends

6020

Arkansas River

50

Texas Creek Store/Cafe

69

Grid size - 0.5 miles

TO SALIDA

TO WESTCLIFFE

© 2007 FunTreks, Inc.

157

Mountain goats not fazed by sight of dirt biker at top of Radical Hill, Trail #19.

Original buildings at west end of St. Elmo.

Cabin at Swandyke Townsite, Trail #19.

Sign register at Empire Hilton cabin.

APPENDIX

Red & White Mountain, Trail #17. Wildflowers in late July.

Other ATV Books/ Maps

All-Terrain Atlas, by All-Terrain Atlas, LLC. Color maps with quality photos and directions to trailhead. Maps are purchased individually and fit into a binder. Trails are marked for Jeeps, ATVs and dirt bikes. Available at www.atamaps.com or at selected ATV and motorcycle stores in Colorado.

ATVing in 14er Country, by Carl Bauer, III, Buena Vista, CO. Forty-page book with 16 ATV trails around the Buena Vista area with maps and historical information. Available at stores in the Buena Vista area.

ATV Riding, published by Tread Lightly!®, Ogden, UT. Small 24-page booklet with ATV riding tips and minimum impact recommendations.

Colorado Atlas & Gazetteer, by Delorme Mapping Company, Yarmouth, ME. Oversize 104-page map atlas of entire state of Colorado. (Revised annually)

Crested Butte/Taylor Park Recreation Topo Map, by Latitude 40° Inc., Nederland, CO. Folded 25″x 39″ two-sided map printed on durable, waterproof material. Incredible detail of 4WD, ATV and single-track routes in the Taylor Park and Crested Butte area. ISBN# 1-879866-23-4. See all their maps at www.latitude40maps.com or call 303-258-7909.

Guide to Colorado Backroads & 4-Wheel Drive Trails, 2nd Edition, by Charles A. Wells, FunTreks Guidebooks, Monument, CO. Book has 286 pages with 75 four-wheel-drive trails (73 for ATVs), 83 maps, over 425 photos, step-by-step directions along the routes and GPS waypoints. ISBN# 0-9664976-6-X. Available at www.funtreks.com, bookstores, selected 4WD shops, ATV and motorcycle stores in Colorado.

Guide to Northern Colorado Backroads & 4-Wheel Drive Trails, by Charles A. Wells, FunTreks Guidebooks, Monument, CO. Book has 192 pages with 45 four-wheel-drive trails (40 for ATVs), 51 maps, over 240 photos, step-by-step directions along the routes and GPS waypoints. ISBN# 0-9664976-8-6. Available at www.funtreks.com, bookstores, selected 4WD shops, ATV and motorcycle stores in Colorado.

Trails of Colorado, ATV Trail Guide, Volumes 1 and 2, by L&M Map & Video Productions, Parker, CO. Each volume is about 60 pages and contains maps, photos and general directions to 10 trail systems in Colorado. This company also has guidebooks and individual maps for dirt bikes. Available at www.lmproductions.com or at selected ATV and motorcycle stores in Colorado.

Trails Illustrated Topo Maps by National Geographic, Evergreen, CO. Quality line of folded maps covering key areas across Colorado. Printed on durable, waterproof material. Available at www.nationalgeographic.com/maps or at stores across Colorado.

Contact Information

ATV Clubs-Colorado

Colorado Quad Runners
Denver, CO
www.cqr.org

Creede OHV Club
804 Starlight Circle
Creede, CO 81130
www.creedeohvclub.com

High Rocky Riders Off Road Club
P. O. Box 1810
Buena Vista, CO 81211
www.highrockyriders.org

Rocky Mountain ATV Club
Castle Rock, CO
www.rockymountainatv.org

Royal Gorge ATV Club
P. O. Box 1311
Canon City, CO 81215
www.royalgorgeatv.com

Thunder Mountain Wheelers
P. O. Box 203
Delta, CO 81416-0203
www.tmwatv.org

Western Slope ATV Association
P. O. Box 4283
Grand Junction, CO 81502-4283
www.wsatva.org

Bureau of Land Management

Web site: www.blm.gov

Colorado State Office
2850 Youngfield Street
Lakewood, CO 80215
(303) 239-3600

Arkansas Headwaters Recreation Area
(State Parks/BLM)
307 West Sackett Ave.
Salida CO 81201
(719) 539-7289

Glenwood Springs Field Office
50629 Highways 6 & 24
Glenwood Springs, CO 81601
(970) 947-2800

Gunnison Field Office
216 N. Colorado Street
Gunnison, CO 81230
(970) 641-0471

Kremmling Field Office
(North Sand Hills)
2103 E. Park Avenue
Kremmling, CO 80459
(970) 724-3000

Royal Gorge Field Office
(BLM/USFS)
3170 East Main Street
Canon City, CO 81212
(719) 269-8500

White River Field Office
73544 Highway 64
Meeker, CO 81641
(970) 878-3800

Chambers of Commerce Visitor Information

Berthoud	(970) 532-4200
Boulder	(303) 442-1044
Breckenridge	(970) 453-2913
Buena Vista	(719) 395-6612
Canon City	(719) 275-2331
Castle Rock	(303) 688-4597
Central City/Blackhawk	(303) 582-3345
Colorado Springs	(719) 635-1551
Cripple Creek	(877) 858-4653
Denver	(303) 534-8500
Dillon (Summit County)	(800) 530-3099
Divide	(719) 687-7670
Estes Park	(800) 378-3708
Evergreen	(303) 674-3412
Fort Collins	(970) 482-3746
Frisco	(970) 668-5547
Georgetown	(303) 569-2405
Golden	(303) 279-3113
Granby	(970) 887-2311
Grand Lake	(970) 627-3402
Idaho Sprgs. (Cleer Crk. Co.)	(303) 567-4660
Leadville	(800) 933-3901
Longmont	(303) 776-5295
Loveland	(970) 667-6311
Lyons	(303) 823-5215
Montezuma (Summit Co.)	(800) 530-3099
Monument (Tri Lakes)	(719) 481-3282
Nederland	(303) 258-3936
Penrose	(719) 372-3994
Pueblo	(719) 542-1704
Salida	(719) 539-2068
Summit County	(800) 530-3099
Vail	(970) 477-0075
Woodland Park	(719) 687-9885
Walden	(970) 723-4600
Winter Park/Fraser	(970) 726-4118

Forest Service

Web site: www.fs.fed.us

Arapaho and Roosevelt National Forest Supervisors Office
2150 Centre Avenue
Building E
Fort Collins, CO 80526-8119
(970) 295-6600

Boulder Ranger District
2140 Yarmouth Avenue
Boulder, CO 80301
(303) 541-2500

Canyon Lakes Ranger District
(Larimer County)
2150 Centre Ave., Building E
Fort Collins, CO 80526
(970) 295-6700

Clear Creek Ranger District & F. S. Visitor Center
101 Chicago Creek Road
P.O. Box 3307
Idaho Springs, CO 80452
(303) 567-3000

Sulphur Ranger District
(Grand County)
P.O. Box 10
9 Ten Mile Drive
Granby, Colorado 80446
(970) 887-4100

Gunnison National Forest Supervisors Office
2250 Highway 50
Delta, CO 81416
(970) 874-6600

Gunnison Ranger District
216 North Colorado
Gunnison, CO 81230
(970) 641-0471

**Pike National Forest and
San Isabel National Forest
Supervisors Office**
2840 Kachina Drive
Pueblo, CO 81008
(719) 553-1400

Leadville Ranger District
810 Front Street
Leadville, CO 80461
(719) 486-0749

Pikes Peak Ranger District
601 South Weber
Colorado Springs, CO 80903
(719) 636-1602

Salida Ranger District
325 West Rainbow Blvd.
Salida, CO 81201
(719) 539-3591

San Carlos Ranger District
3170 East Main Street
Canon City, CO 81212
(719) 269-8500

South Park Ranger District
P.O. Box 219, 320 Hwy. 285
Fairplay, CO 80440
(719) 836-2031

South Platte Ranger District
(SW Denver, Rampart Range)
19316 Goddard Ranch Court
Morrison, CO 80465
(303) 275-5610

**Rio Grande National Forest
Supervisors Office**
1803 W. Highway 160
Monte Vista, CO 81144
(719) 852-5941

Saguache Ranger District
P. O. Box 67
46525 State Hwy. 114
Saguache, CO 81149
(719) 655-2553

**White River National Forest
Supervisors Office**
P.O. Box 948
900 Grand Avenue
Glenwood Springs, CO 81602
(970) 945-2521

Dillon Ranger District
P.O. Box 620
680 Blue River Parkway
Silverthorne, CO 80498
(970) 468-5400

Holy Cross Ranger District
(Vail, Camp Hale area)
P.O. Box 190
24747 US Highway 24
Minturn, CO 81645
(970) 827-5715

GPS/Map Sources

Delorme Mapping
P.O. Box 298
Yarmouth, ME 04096
(800) 561-5105
www.delorme.com

Garmin International
1200 E. 151st Street
Olathe, KS 66062
(800) 800-1020
www.garmin.com

GPS NOW
www.GPSNOW.com

Latitude 40°, Inc.
P. O. Box 189
Nederland,
Boulder County, CO 80466
(303) 258-7909
www.latitude40maps.com

National Geographic Maps
P.O. Box 4357
Evergreen, CO 80437
(800) 962-1643
www.nationalgeographic.com/maps

Ram Mounts
(mounts for GPS units)
(206) 763-8361
www.ram-mount.com

OHV Support Organizations

ATVA
All-Terrain Vehicle Association
13515 Yarmouth Drive
Pickerington, OH 43147
(866) 288-2564
www.atvaonline.com

COHVCO
Colorado Off Highway Vehicle Coalition
P.O. Box 620523
Littleton, CO 80162
(303) 539-5010
www.cohvco.org

Stay the Trail
P.O. Box 620523
Littleton, CO 80162
www.staythetrail.org

Blue Ribbon Coalition
4555 Burley Drive Ste. A
Pocatello, ID 83202-1921
(800) 258-3742
www.sharetrails.org
`

Colorado Association of 4-Wheel Drive Clubs, Inc.
P.O. Box 1413
Wheat Ridge, CO 80034
(303) 857-7992
www.hightrails.org

United Four Wheel Drive Associations
7135 S. PR Royal Springs Drive
Shelbyville, IN 46176
(800) 448-3932
www.ufwda.org

OHV Registration

Colorado State Parks
OHV registration information
13787 S. Highway 85
Littleton, CO 80125
(303) 791-1920
www.parks.state.co.us

Other Helpful Contacts

ATV clubs across the entire United States
www.atvsource.com

ATV Safety Institute
2 Jenner Street, Suite 150
Irvine, CA 92618-3806
(800) 887-2887
www.atvsafety.org

Bugling Bull Trading Post
(near Rampart Range OHV Area)
1668 N. Highway 67
Sedalia, CO 80135
(303) 688-9701

Colorado State Forest State Park & Moose Visitor Center
56750 Highway 14
Walden, CO 80480
(970) 723-8366
www.parks.state.co.us

National Forest Camping Reservations
(877) 444-6777
www.recreation.gov

North Sand Hills
www.co.blm.gov/kra/NorthSand
HillSRMA.htm

NOVA Guides
P. O. Box 2018
Vail, CO 81658
(719) 486-2656
www.novaguides.com

Rampart Range Motorcycle Management Committee
P. O. Box 3511
Englewood, CO 80155
www.rampartrange.org

Sprucewood Inn
(near Rampart Range OHV Area)
491 S. Highway 67
Sedalia, CO 80135
(303) 688-3231

St. Elmo General Store, Inc.
P. O. Box 158
Nathrop, CO 81236
(719) 395-2117
www.st-elmo.com

Wag Bags®
Portable Environmental
Toilet System
www.thepett.com

About the Author

Charles A. Wells graduated from Ohio State University in 1969 with a degree in graphic design. After practicing design in Ohio, he moved to Colorado Springs in 1980 and worked 18 years in the printing business. Over the years, he and his family enjoyed a wide array of outdoor activities including hiking, biking, rafting and skiing. He bought an SUV in 1994 and immediately got addicted to exploring Colorado's remote backcountry. He later joined a four-wheel-drive club and learned about hardcore four-wheeling.

Dissatisfied with the four-wheel-drive guidebooks on the market, he decided to write his own. His first book on Colorado sold well enough for him to leave his regular job to write full time. He later fell in love with Moab and returned year after year. He presently has six SUV/Jeeping books on the market—two on Colorado, one on Moab, one on Arizona and two on California. More are planned.

He noticed sales of his Jeeping books were increasing at ATV stores with more customers calling to ask which trails allowed ATVs. He began including ATV information in his regular books. Seeing more and more ATVs on the trails, he decided to try it himself and quickly got hooked. He bought his own ATV and began riding more frequently and now has two books exclusively for ATVs.

This book is second in a series of quality guidebooks for ATV enthusiasts. A new, simpler, full-color format has been designed based on what the author has learned on the trails. Let him know what you think. Check www.funtreks.com for more ATV books in the future.

Author at the door to the Empire Hilton cabin on the Bill Moore Lake, Empire Loop, Trail #14. Anyone can stay in the cabin if it is not already occupied.

Order Form

Order 4 ways: (We accept Visa, Mastercard, Discover, American Express)
1. Call toll-free **1-877-222-7623**
2. Online at www.funtreks.com (secure site)
3. By Mail: Send this completed order form to:
   FunTreks, Inc, P. O. Box 3127, Monument, CO 80132
4. Fax this completed order form to 719-277-7411.

Please send me the following book(s): (I understand that if I am not completely satisfied, I may return the book(s) for a full refund, no questions asked.)

Qty.

ATV Trails Guide, Colorado Central Mountains (full color)
ISBN 0-9664976-9-4, 168 pages, Price $19.95 _____

ATV Trails Guide, Moab, UT (full color)
ISBN 0-9664976-7-8, 160 pages, Price $18.95 _____

Guide to Colorado Backroads & 4-Wheel Drive Trails (2nd Edition)
ISBN 0-9664976-6-X, 286 pages, Price $24.95 _____

Guide to Northern Colorado Backroads & 4-Wheel Drive Trails
ISBN 0-9664976-8-6, 192 pages, Price $19.95 _____

Guide to Moab, UT Backroads & 4-Wheel Drive Trails
ISBN 0-9664976-2-7, 268 pages, Price $24.95 _____

Guide to Arizona Backroads & 4-Wheel Drive Trails
ISBN 0-9664976-3-5, 286 pages, Price $24.95 _____

Guide to Southern California Backroads & 4-Wheel Drive Trails
ISBN 0-9664976-4-3, 286 pages, Price $24.95 _____

Guide to Northern California Backroads & 4-Wheel Drive Trails
ISBN 0-9664976-5-1, 286 pages, Price $24.95 _____

Name: (please print)_____
Address:_____
City:_____ State:____ Zip:_____
Telephone: (_____) _____-_____

Sales Tax: Colorado residents add 2.9%. (Subject to change without notice.)
Shipping: $4.50 for first book and $1.00 for each additional book.

Payment Method: Check one:
_____ Check
_____ Visa
_____ Mastercard   Card number:_____
_____ Discover   Expiration Date:_____
_____ American Express   Name on card:_____

Thanks for your order.

Other books by Charles A. Wells

In addition to Charles Wells' two ATV books, many ATV enthusiasts rely on his 4-wheel-drive books. His two Colorado books combined, contain another 72 ATV trails not included in this book. His 4-wheel-drive books are black and white inside and are in a different format, but include clear directions, a map for each trail, hundreds of photos and GPS waypoints.

ATV Trails Guide Moab, UT
(Full color throughout)
30 trails, 195 photos, 31 maps, GPS waypoints, 5.5˝x 8.5,˝ 160 pages, $18.95, ISBN 0-9664976-7-8

Guide to Colorado Backroads & 4-Wheel Drive Trails (2nd Edition)
73 ATV trails, 75 total trails, over 425 photos, 83 maps, 6˝x 9,˝ GPS waypoints, 286 pages, $24.95, ISBN 0-9664976-6-X

Guide to Northern Colorado Backroads & 4-Wheel Drive Trails
40 ATV trails, 45 total trails, over 240 photos, 51 maps, 6˝x 9,˝ GPS waypoints, 192 pages, $19.95, ISBN 0-9664976-8-6

Guide to Moab, UT Backroads & 4-Wheel Drive Trails
27 ATV trails, 50 total trails, over 245 photos, 55 maps, 6˝x 9,˝ GPS waypoints, 268 pages, $24.95, ISBN 0-9664976-2-7

Guide to Arizona Backroads & 4-Wheel Drive Trails
38 ATV trails, 75 total trails, over 300 photos, 86 maps, 6˝x 9,˝ GPS waypoints, 286 pages, $24.95, ISBN 0-9664976-3-5

Guide to Southern California Backroads & 4-Wheel-Drive Trails
39 ATV trails, 75 total trails, over 340 photos, 86 maps, 6˝x 9,˝ GPS waypoints, 286 pages, $24.95, ISBN 0-9664976-4-3

Guide to Northern California Backroads & 4-Wheel-Drive Trails
65 ATV trails, 75 total trails, over 400 photos, 85 maps, 6˝x 9,˝ GPS waypoints, 286 pages, $24.95, ISBN 0-9664976-5-1

To order, call toll-free 877-222-7623 or visit our Web site at www.funtreks.com